KWIK·SEW®'S
SEWING FOR CHILDREN

by Kerstin Martensson

ISBN 0-913212-17-2

456789

About the Author

KERSTIN MARTENSSON was born in Göteborg, Sweden. She was educated in clothing construction, pattern design and fashion, completing studies in both Sweden and England. After completing her education, Kerstin relocated to Minneapolis, Minnesota where she founded KWIK•SEW Pattern Company in 1967. She dedicated herself to creating quality patterns for the home sewer, offering the latest fashions and sewing techniques. Kerstin also traveled extensively throughout the United States, Canada, Australia and Europe, earning international recognition by sharing her methods for making sewing faster, easier and more fun.

KWIK•SEW'S SEWING FOR CHILDREN is one of a collection of home sewing books published by KWIK•SEW. These books have achieved global success that can be attributed to their illustrated, easy to follow step-by-step instructions. To date, more than two million copies have been sold—many being used by schools and colleges as sewing textbooks.

KWIK•SEW Pattern Company continues to uphold Kerstin Martensson's dedication to the home sewer by providing quality patterns, as well as sewing books, that are easy to use. Today there are more than 800 KWIK•SEW patterns to choose from, including the latest fashions and variety of crafts. The company has also expanded to world-wide operation and distribution. To learn more about KWIK•SEW, visit the company website www.kwiksew.com.

Introduction

Sewing for children can be a very rewarding experience in many ways. It gives you an opportunity to be creative with appliqués and color blocking. At this age children usually want to dress like their friends, yet they are developing definite tastes of their own and want to show some degree of individuality. They want a sweatshirt like their friends, however, the use of color blocking can turn that garment into something special, it will still be a sweatshirt, but it is their sweatshirt.

When you are sewing for children, try, if possible, to get them interested in the project, get them involved by taking them with you when you purchase the fabric. If they choose a particular design or color, they are more likely to love the garment and want to wear it more often. Some children may express a desire to pick out or design their own appliqués, like you, they also have a desire to be creative. Maybe the first item will not be the perfect garment you envisioned, but you have started them on what could be a rewarding hobby that will last them a lifetime. Older children, with your guidance, may want to sew some of the seams themselves. Help them by encouraging them and try not to be critical, after all they are the ones who will be wearing the clothes. Try to make it a fun project so that you both enjoy it. This not only applies to girls, but also to boys, many boys are just as interested as girls and in addition, they may be fascinated by the sewing machine itself. How does the machine work? How does the needle pick up the thread?

In addition to the fun you will have sewing for children, an additional reward is the money you will save. Most people believe that as children's clothes are much smaller than adult's clothing, they are also less expensive. This is not the case, while they may be somewhat less expensive, children's clothes cost a lot of money when they are purchased in your local store.

This book has been written with the help of all the skilled staff in the Design and Art Departments of KWIK•SEW Pattern Company. Their combined talents have resulted in a book that is up-to-date, full of creative ideas and illustrations.

T-shirt dress, Self fabric neckband and cuffs. Headband with bow.

Basic T-shirt, Neckband with contrast inset, Basic shorts, Pockets in side seams.

Contents

General Information

FABRIC

When choosing fabrics for children's clothes, it is very important that you select fabrics which are washable and colorfast, one garment that runs could ruin an entire wash. When purchasing fabric, be sure to allow extra fabric for shrinkage, usually all fabrics with cotton will shrink to some degree. When the fabric has a design or stripes, allow extra fabric in order to match the stripes or designs. Before you cut out any garment, we recommend that you pre-wash the fabric. Do not pre-wash ribbing as this makes it difficult to sew.

For children's clothes you will be using a variety of fabrics, both knit and woven. Knit fabrics such as single knit, interlock, stretch velour with approximately 20% - 25% stretch across the grain. Firm knits with a very small amount of stretch such as double knits, sweatshirt fleece, and some velour. Woven fabrics such as broadcloth, chambray, sheeting, seersucker, twill, corduroy, lightweight denim and windbreaker fabric.

If using knit fabrics, it is important to use fabric with the recommended degree of stretch. For example, if the recommended fabric is a single knit with 20% stretch and you use an interlock with 25% stretch, the garment will have a looser fit. If the fabric stretches less, the garment will have a closer fit. You should not substitute a woven fabric for a knit fabric or use a knit fabric when the pattern recommends only woven fabrics. Some patterns are designed for both woven and knit fabric, but these knits should be firm and have a small degree of stretch. For neckbands, waistband and cuffs, we recommend using ribbing with 100% stretch.

When using knit fabric, test the fabric for the degree of stretch. Fold over the crosswise edge of the fabric approximately 3" (8 cm) and mark 4" (10 cm) with pins. Hold the 4" (10 cm) of the folded fabric against the chart and gently stretch it to the outside line. If the fabric stretches easily, without excessive rolling, to this line or slightly farther, the fabric has the correct amount of stretch for the pattern. This is also a good time to check the fabric for recovery, if the fabric does not return to its original shape after being stretched, it will probably mean that the fabric will sag and stretch out of shape when the garment is worn.

Shirt with front placket and faced neckline, Flared shorts, Pockets in side seams.

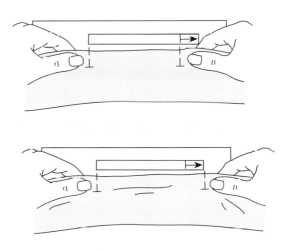

STRETCH CHARTS

Fabric with 20% stretch across the grain such as: Single knit, Double knit, Interlock

| 4" of Knit Fabric should stretch | to at least here. → |

Fabric with 25% stretch across the grain such as: Interlock, Velour

| 4" of Knit Fabric should stretch | to at least here → |

Fabric with 100% stretch across the grain such as: Ribbing

| 4" of Knit Fabric should stretch | to at least here. → |

PATTERNS

Inside the back cover of this book is a Master pattern for children, approximately four to twelve years of age. This is a unisex pattern to fit both boys and girls. The Master pattern includes T-shirts, Tops, Sweatshirts, Jackets, Pants, Shorts, and many variations.

If you would like to have additional designs for children which are not included in the Master pattern, you can obtain KWIK•SEW Patterns at your local fabric store. Kwik Sew has a large selection of Children's patterns, as well as patterns for all other types of sewing.

The Master pattern is printed on both sides of the paper and the pattern pieces have to be traced. Each size is printed in a different color to make it easy to follow when tracing. To trace the pattern, use tracing paper or a tracing cloth which is made from pressed fibers. This cloth is durable and will not tear, it is also transparent for easy tracing. Trace the pattern pieces for the size you have selected and be sure to follow the same size on all the pattern pieces.

All the pattern pieces have a ¼" (6 mm) seam allowance included, unless otherwise indicated in the step-by-step instructions.

To make it easier for you to select the correct pattern pieces, each one is numbered and identified.

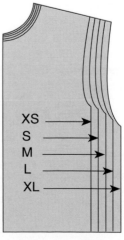

MASTER PATTERN PIECES

1. T-shirt Front
2. T-shirt Back
3. T-shirt Sleeve
4. T-shirt Neckband
5. T-shirt Pocket
6. T-shirt Waistband
7. T-shirt Placket
8. T-shirt Back Neckline Facing
9. T-shirt Upper Collar
10. T-shirt Under Collar
11. T-shirt Back Neckline Binding
12. T-shirt Collar
13. Sweatshirt Front
14. Sweatshirt Back
15. Sweatshirt Sleeve
16. Sweatshirt Neckband
17. Sweatshirt Cuff
18. Sweatshirt Kangaroo Pocket
19. Sweatshirt Hood
20. Sweatshirt Neckline Binding
21. Sweatshirt Collar
22. Sweatshirt Side Pocket
23. Sweatshirt Overlapped Neckband
24. Welt Pocket
25. Pants Front
26. Pants Back
27. Pants Pocket

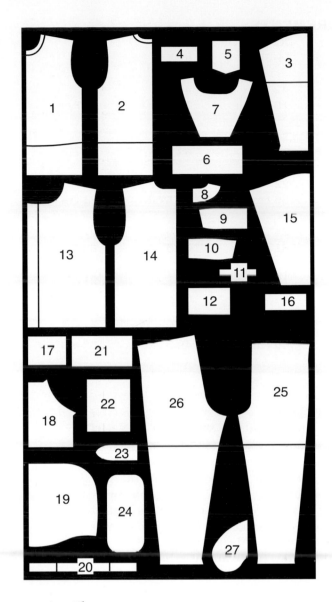

CHOOSING SIZE

Patterns are made to fit specific body measurements with ease allowed for comfort and style. Before you trace the pattern, it is necessary to determine which size to use. Because children differ so much in size, even though they are the same age, be sure to measure the child's height, chest, waist, hip, and shoulder and arm length. For the chest and the hip, measure around the fullest part, and for the waist, measure around the natural waist. For the correct height, measure the child without shoes, standing against a wall. For the shoulder and arm length, measure from the base of the neck, with the arm slightly bent over the shoulder to the wrist.

Choose the size by comparing their height to the height given on Page 8. Choose the size that is closest to their height, then compare the chest, waist and the hip measurements. If in between sizes, choose the larger size. Measure the child for the correct length of the particular garment you are making. The finished lengths of the garments are given in each section. The finished widths of the garments are given on the Master pattern pieces.

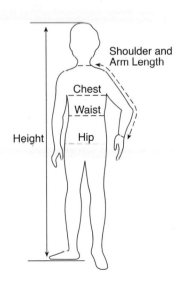

BODY MEASUREMENTS

UNISEX SIZES	XS	S	M	L	XL
(Age)	(4-5)	(6)	(7-8)	(10)	(12)
Height	42"	46"	50"	54"	58"
	107 cm	117 cm	127 cm	137 cm	147 cm
Chest	24"	25"	26½"	28"	30"
	61 cm	63.5 cm	67 cm	71 cm	76 cm
Waist	22"	23"	24"	25"	26"
	56 cm	58.5 cm	61 cm	63.5 cm	66 cm
Hip	24"	25"	27"	29"	31"
	61 cm	63.5 cm	68.5 cm	73.5 cm	78.5 cm
Inside leg to floor	16½"	19"	21½"	24"	26"
	42 cm	48 cm	54.5 cm	61 cm	66 cm
Shoulder and arm length	18"	19½"	21"	23"	25"
	46 cm	49.5 cm	53 cm	58 cm	63 cm

ADJUSTING LENGTH

The most common adjustment that you make on a pattern is the length. You may want to either lengthen or shorten the pattern. The Master pattern pieces have lines indicating where to shorten or lengthen the pattern. Cut the pattern apart on this line, adjust the length by overlapping the pattern to shorten the pattern or tape a strip of paper between the two pieces equal to the amount you want to lengthen the pattern. Make sure to do the same adjustments on both the front and the back pattern pieces. For the correct sleeve length, compare the shoulder and arm length given above to the child's measurement, and shorten or lengthen the sleeve if necessary.

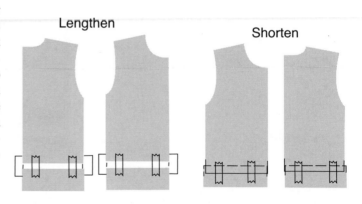

Lengthen   Shorten

ADJUSTING WIDTH

If you need to change the width of the shirt, determine the amount of adjustment needed and divide by four. Draw a line on the front and the back from the shoulder to the bottom edge. This line should be parallel to the grain line. Cut the pattern apart on this line. Spread the pattern apart to make it larger and overlap to make it smaller. Be sure to make the same adjustments on the front and the back pattern pieces. Redraw the shoulder. This adjustment will change the finished length of the shoulder and sleeve. Be sure to check the sleeve length and adjust if necessary.

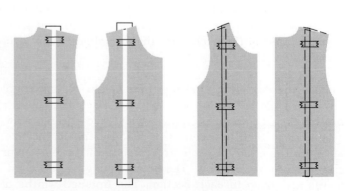

If you need to change the width of the pants, determine the amount of adjustment needed and divide by four. On the front and the back, draw a line perpendicular to the grain line 3" (8 cm) below the crotch. Draw a line parallel to the grain line from the waist to this line. Cut the pattern apart on the line. Spread the pattern apart to make it larger and overlap to make it smaller. Be sure to make the same adjustments on the front and the back pattern pieces. Draw smooth connecting lines on the outside and the inside leg seams.

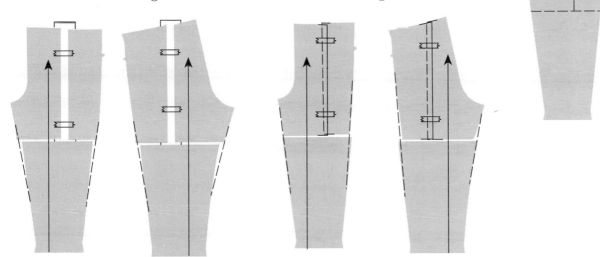

CUTTING

When cutting any type of fabric, it is very important to use a pair of sharp scissors to obtain a clean cut. Dull scissors have a tendency to chew the fabric rather than cut it. If they should become dull, get them sharpened as soon as possible.

The usual procedure for cutting is to fold the fabric double, right sides together. If you are using a striped fabric, be sure to line up the stripes. Layouts are given for the basic garments, if using a variation, use the layouts only as a guide.

Some fabrics are often doubled when put on a bolt, and have a crease at the fold. Before cutting, try to press out this crease. If you are unable to press out the crease, refold the fabric so that the crease is not in a conspicuous place.

Place all the pattern pieces on the fabric before you start cutting. Be sure to follow the grain line and if using stretch fabric, be sure to place the pattern pieces with the stretch going around the body. Pin the pattern pieces to the fabric, or use weights to hold the pattern pieces in place. Cut out the pattern pieces. After cutting out the pattern pieces, mark each piece so you do not mix them up. We recommend using transparent tape, place a small piece on the wrong side of the fabric, marking the side seams, back, etc. Use tape that has a dull finish which you can write on. Always use a pencil, as a ball point pen could spot the fabric and ink is difficult to wash out.

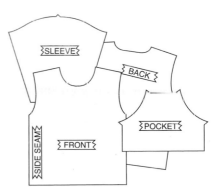

Rather than using notches to mark the center front, center back and the folding lines, it is easier to make tiny clips on the seam allowance. Clip only ⅛" (3 mm), these clips are more accurate and much faster to make. Clips cannot be used on some fabrics such as sweater or loosely woven fabrics as they would be impossible to find.

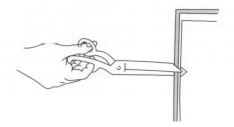

LAYOUT CODE

The following layout codes are used:

 Fabric

 Pattern Piece

If a pattern piece is marked "Place on Fold" and is shown in the following manner, cut all the other pattern pieces first, allowing fabric where the shaded half is shown. Then fold the fabric and cut the piece on the fold.

Fold

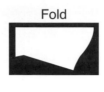

THREAD

The most common thread you will be using is an all purpose thread. It can be cotton, cotton wrapped with polyester, or polyester thread. Always use the same thread for the bobbin and the top thread. If you are unable to find a color thread exactly the same as the color of the fabric, choose a slightly lighter shade, this will blend better than the darker shade.

Threads for serger (overlock) machines are available in large and small tubes and cones. Choose a good quality lightweight thread to make the seams less bulky. The serger thread does not necessarily have to match the garment, you can combine different colors of thread to make them blend with the fabric.

INTERFACING

Interfacing is used to support and shape details such as collars, pockets, and under button and snap closures. Interfacing is available in fusible and sew on kind, in different weights and colors. It is much easier to use fusible interfacing, and it can be used on most fabrics. Choose the interfacing according to the weight of the fabric and the shaping needed. Always test your interfacing on a scrap of the same fabric you are using, to see if the result is satisfactory. Fusible knit interfacing works well on lightweight knit or woven fabrics. If you wish to have a little more support, we recommend using a woven fusible interfacing from a blend of polyester and rayon. When applying fusible interfacing, follow the manufacturers directions.

SEAMS & SEAM FINISHES

The type of stitch you will use to sew the seams will depend upon the type of fabric you are using, and the type of sewing machine you have.

Before you start sewing the garment, take a small piece of scrap fabric that your garment is cut from, double the fabric and sew a straight stitch. Check the stitches to be sure the tensions are correct. The perfect thread tension results when the top and the bottom tensions are exactly equal and the knot cannot be seen. The best rule to follow, is to adjust the tensions so that the stitch appears the same on both sides. See illustration. Try to adjust only the top tension as this is easier to do on all sewing machines, however, in some cases you may have to adjust both the top and the bottom tensions.

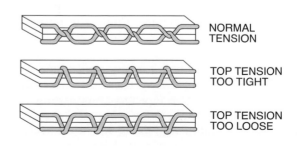

NORMAL TENSION

TOP TENSION TOO TIGHT

TOP TENSION TOO LOOSE

You will find it much easier to start a seam if you lower the needle into the fabric and hold both the top and bottom threads in your hand behind the presser foot. As the machine starts to sew, slowly pull these threads toward the rear of the machine. This will help the machine feed the fabric and eliminate the tendency of the fabric to bunch up under the presser foot.

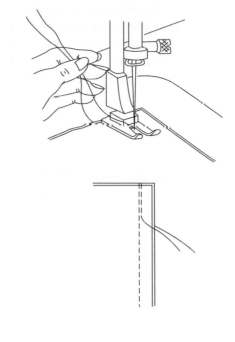

Most of the time when you start a seam, you will want to lock the seam. This is done by starting the seam in from the edge of the fabric. Sew a few stitches in reverse and then continue the seam in the usual manner.

TO MAKE A SEAM
Pin two pieces of fabric, right sides and raw edges together, unless otherwise specified in the instructions, and sew, using the seam allowance indicated.

STITCH LENGTH
Instructions refer to stitch length as short, medium and long. The number of stitches per inch or centimeter determines the stitch length.

Short	12-20 stitches per inch
	6-8 stitches per centimeter
Medium	10-12 stitches per inch
	4-5 stitches per centimeter
Long	4-8 stitches per inch
	2-3 stitches per centimeter
Satin Stitching	35-50 stitches per inch
	15-20 stitches per centimeter

SEAMS FOR KNIT FABRIC
USING 1/4" (6 mm) SEAM ALLOWANCE

REVERSE CYCLE MACHINE
Sew the seam, using an overlock stitch. This stitch sews and overcasts in one step. It is not necessary to stretch the fabric while sewing, as this is an elastic seam.

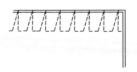

ZIGZAG MACHINE
Sew the seams with a narrow zigzag width and a medium stitch length. This seam will stretch with the fabric. Overcast the seam allowances together with a large zigzag stitch or you can use a three-step zigzag stitch.

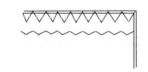 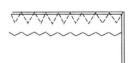

STRAIGHT STITCH MACHINE
Sew the seam, using a medium stitch length; stretch the fabric in the front and in the back of the presser foot as you sew. Sew another seam on the seam allowance close to the raw edges to keep seam allowances together.

SERGER (OVERLOCK) MACHINE

This type of sewing machine gives a very professional look. Serger (overlock) machines sew, overcast and trim the excess seam allowance in one step. When using a serger (overlock) machine, be sure that you are using the correct seam allowance so the garment will fit properly.

Serger (overlock) machines will not sew over pins. Pin only when necessary and remove the pins well ahead of the knife or pin far over to the left of the cut edges and remove the pins after the seam is completed.

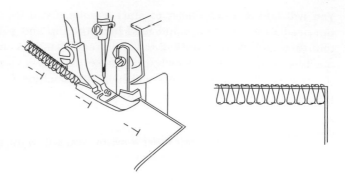

SEAMS FOR WOVEN FABRIC
USING 1/4" (6 mm) SEAM ALLOWANCE

For woven fabric, sew the seams, using a medium length straight stitch. Overcast the raw edges, using a medium zigzag stitch, three-step zigzag stitch, sew a straight stitch close to the edges, or use a serger (overlock) machine.

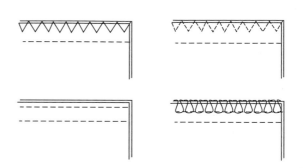

SEWING TERMS

The following sewing terms, are used in this book and also in the pattern instruction sheets. The sewing terms tell you what to do, but do not give the procedures in the step-by-step instructions.

UNDER STITCHING

Under stitching is straight stitching the seam allowance to the facing to prevent the seam and the facing from rolling to the outside of the garment. Before under stitching, clip curved seam allowance. Fold the seam allowance toward the facing as you are sewing on the facing close to the seam. Trim the seam allowance close to the stitches.

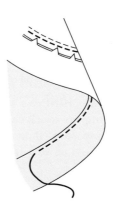

STITCH IN THE DITCH

Stitching in the ditch is straight stitching on the right side of the garment, close to the seam. It is used to secure collars, facings and bindings. This stitching will not be readily visible if done carefully. On the right side of the garment, sew as close as possible to the seam, using a zipper foot.

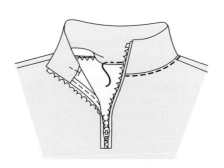

EASING AND GATHERING

One or two rows of straight stitching with a long stitch length and looser upper thread tension. Sew on the seam line and again in the middle of the seam allowance. To gather, pull the threads and secure by wrapping around a pin as shown.

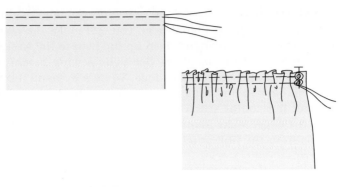

STAY STITCHING

Stay stitching is straight stitching on the seam line or curved areas, such as on a pocket and a neckline, and it prevents these areas from stretching while handling. It is also used for corners where clipping the seam allowance to the seam will be necessary, in this case, use a short stitch length.

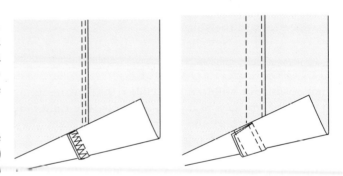

TOPSTITCHING

Topstitching can be decorative as well as functional. Most topstitching is done with a straight stitch. You can use the same color thread as used for the garment or a contrasting thread. You can use a single or double needle. See your sewing machine manual for using a double needle.

Topstitching ¼" (6 mm) or wider from a seam will require a ⅝" (1.5 cm) seam allowance. Be sure to add ⅜" (1 cm) to the seams when cutting out the pattern pieces. Press the seam allowance to one side and topstitch close to the seam and again ¼" (6 mm) from the first topstitching.

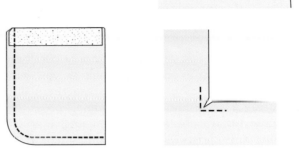

HEMMING

A topstitched hem is the easiest way to hem children's clothes. Overcast the raw edge, fold the hem to the wrong side and press. Sew the hem, with a straight stitch or a narrow zigzag width and a medium stitch length, close to the overcasted edge.

An attractive finish can be obtained, if you use a double needle and sew the hem from the right side. Refer to your sewing machine manual for using a double needle.

For narrow hems, overcast the edge, fold ¼" (6 mm) to the wrong side and press. Sew close to the inner edge of the hem. If using a lightweight woven fabric, make a double narrow hem, fold ⅛" (3 mm) to the wrong side and sew the seam. Press the hem. Fold again along the raw edge and sew another seam.

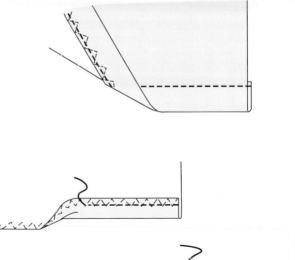

BLIND HEMS

If you prefer to have a blind hem, you can make the hem on the machine or by hand. Fold up the hem to the wrong side, press and pin in place. See your sewing machine manual for blind hem instructions. To hem by hand, turn the hem back and working from the left to the right, make a small horizontal stitch on the garment ¼" (6 mm) in from the edge. Make another stitch in the hem diagonally across from the first stitch. Make the stitches in a zigzag pattern.

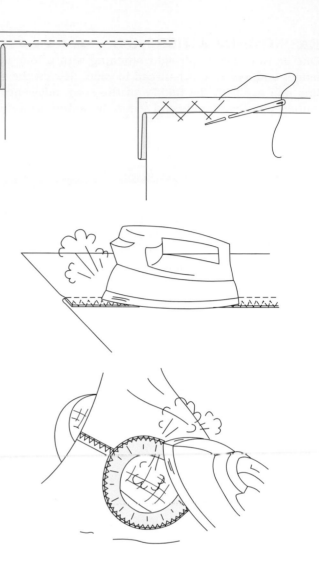

PRESSING

It is very important to press the seams as you sew them. After sewing the seams, always press them flat first. When using a ¼" (6 mm) seam allowance, press the seam allowances toward one side. When using a ⅝" (1.5 cm) seam allowance, press the seams open.

To obtain a professional looking neckline, it is very important to press the neckline after you have sewn the neckband. Place the neckline over a pressing ham and steam press the neckline into shape, pressing the seam allowance toward the shirt.

BUTTONS & BUTTONHOLES

When sewing for children, remember that garments overlap different for boys and girls. For girls, the right side of the garment overlaps the left side, and for boys, the left side overlaps the right side.

Buttonholes should be ⅛" (2 mm) larger than the buttons. If you are making vertical buttonholes, mark the placement along the center front. If you are making horizontal buttonholes, start the buttonhole ⅛" (2 mm) from the center front toward the edge of the garment. When making the buttonholes, refer to your sewing machine manual. Always sew on the buttons along the center front on the other side of the garment. Buttons can be sewn on by hand or by machine, refer to your sewing machine manual. Instead of buttons and buttonholes, you can use snaps.

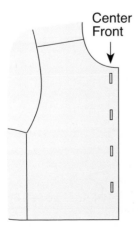

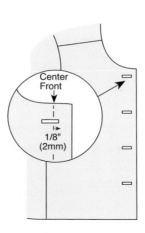

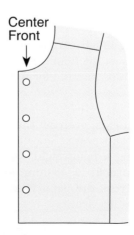

T-shirts & Tops

If any garment could be classified as a child's uniform, it is a T-shirt. Fortunately, it is one of the easiest garment to make and coupled with a pair of shorts or pants you have a complete outfit. T-shirts can be adapted for any season or climate by using long or short sleeves and by using lightweight or heavier weight fabric.

Even though T-shirts are easy to make, they are still very expensive to buy in a children's ready-to-wear store. This is one garment that will save you money, if you make it yourself, as children of all ages seem to require so many of them. In addition to saving you money, it will give you and your child a wonderful opportunity to be creative as it is perfect for appliqués or color blocking.

For the T-shirt, use single knit, jersey, interlock, or textured lightweight knit. The fabric should have approximately 20% stretch across the grain. Interlock sometimes has more than 20% stretch, if using a fabric with more stretch, the garment will have a looser fit.

For the cuffs and the neckband, we recommend using ribbing with 100% stretch across the grain. However, some ribbings have more stretch and some have less. Keep in mind, that the lengths of the bands might have to be adjusted. Most ribbings which are very soft need to be shortened and ribbings which are heavy and firm need to be lengthened. Make sure to check the stretch of your fabric and ribbing with the stretch charts on Page 5.

This section includes instructions for a basic T-shirt. Variations of this basic shirt include neck finishes such as placket with collar, front placket and faced neckline, collar with front zipper and yoke with opening. Variations of sleeve finishes include cuffs and roll-up sleeves. Hem finishes include ribbing waistband, drawstring and hemline slits. More styles can be obtained by combining the neckline and the hem finishes.

For selecting the size and making adjustments on the pattern, see Pages 7 and 8.

The following is the finished length of the T-shirt at the center back:

XS	S	M	L	XL
16¾"	18"	19¼"	20¾"	22¼"
42 cm	45 cm	49 cm	52 cm	56 cm

Compare the finished length to the length you wish the shirt to be, and make the necessary adjustments on the pattern pieces.

Basic T-shirt, Pocket, Shorts, Pockets in side seams, Stitched waist elastic.

BASIC T-SHIRT

The Basic T-shirt has a crew neckline with ribbing neck-band, hemmed bottom edge and hemmed long or short sleeves.

Use Master pattern pieces:
1. T-shirt Front
2. T-shirt Back
3. T-shirt Sleeve
4. T-shirt Neckband

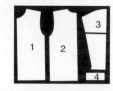

Decide if you want to have long or short sleeves. Trace the pattern pieces, following **neckline A** on the front and the back.

Fold the fabric double with the right sides together. Place the pattern pieces on the fabric, following the layouts. Be sure to always follow the arrows on the pattern pieces for the correct grain and stretch of the fabric. Cut out the front, back and the sleeves. The pattern piece for the sleeve has to be used twice and placed on the fold to obtain two sleeves. Cut out the neckband from ribbing.

It is a good idea to stabilize the shoulder seams, you can use fusible interfacing or strips of the self fabric. Cut two pieces on the lengthwise grain ½" (1.3 cm) wide and the length of the shoulder. Pin the stabilizing strips to the wrong side of the front shoulders, or if using fusible inter-facing, fuse to the wrong side. Sew the front to the back at the shoulder seams, and press the seams toward the back.

Finish the neckline before you proceed with the rest of the garment. Sew the ends of the neckband, right sides together, with a straight stitch and press the seam allowance open. Fold the neckband double lengthwise, wrong sides and raw edges together. Divide the neckband and the neckline into fourths with pins, placing the pins at the center back, center front, and an equal distance between the pins. NOTE: The pins will not be at the shoulder seams.

Pin the neckband to the right side of the neckline with all the raw edges together, matching the pins and the seam on the neckband to the center back. When sewing the neckband, stretch the neckband between the pins to fit the neckline. The easiest way to do this is to have the smallest piece on top. In this case, the neckline is under-neath and the neckband is on top.

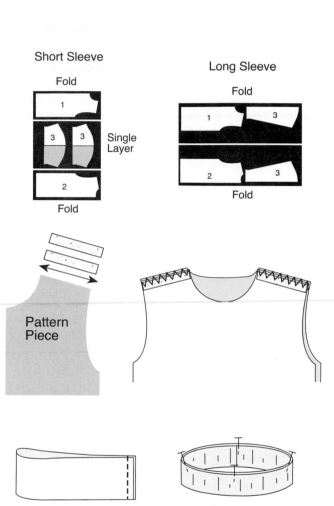

Short Sleeve

Long Sleeve

Single Layer

Pattern Piece

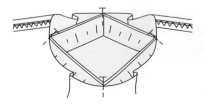

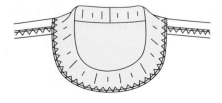

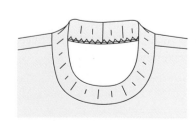

If desired, topstitch the neckline close to the neckline seam, using a narrow zigzag stitch or a double needle.

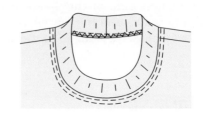

Pin the sleeves to the armholes, right sides together. The left and the right sleeves are identical. Match the notch on the sleeve to the shoulder seam and the underarm edges even. Sew the sleeves in place.

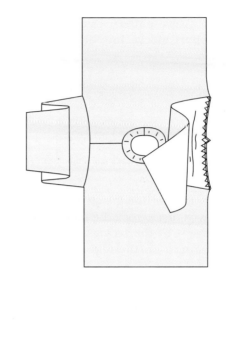

Pin the back to the front, right sides together, at the side seams and the sleeve seams, matching the underarm seams. Sew the side seam and the sleeve seam in one continuous step, starting at the bottom of the shirt.

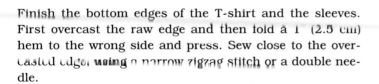

Finish the bottom edges of the T-shirt and the sleeves. First overcast the raw edge and then fold a 1" (2.5 cm) hem to the wrong side and press. Sew close to the over-casted edge, using a narrow zigzag stitch or a double needle.

CUFFS

If you wish, you may have cuffs on the long sleeves. Use Master pattern piece 17 for the cuffs and cut two from ribbing.

Shorten the sleeve pattern piece 2" (5 cm) at the bottom edge, as the cuffs will add to the length of the sleeves.

Sew the sleeve seams of the cuffs, right sides together, matching the notches; use a straight stitch and press the seams open. Fold each cuff double, wrong sides and raw edges together. Divide the cuffs and the sleeve openings in half with pins.

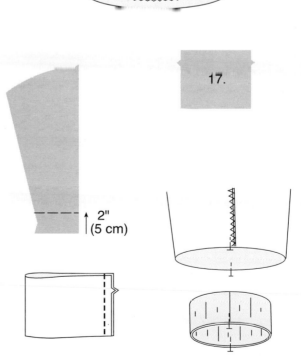

17.

Pin the cuffs to the right side of the sleeve openings, matching the pins, the seams and the raw edges together. Sew on the cuffs, stretching the cuffs to fit the openings.

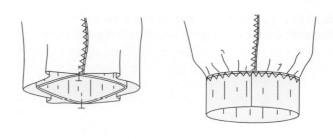

SHORT ROLL-UP SLEEVES

A short roll-up sleeve is a very attractive way to finish the sleeves, especially if you use a contrasting fabric for the facing. Lengthen the sleeve pattern piece 1½" (4 cm) at the bottom of the short sleeve line and eliminate the extension for the hem.

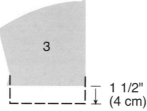

To make the pattern piece for the facing, trace the bottom of the sleeve and draw a line across the pattern 4" (10 cm) above the bottom edge. Cut the facings from contrasting fabric, placing the pattern on the fold of the fabric and cut two.

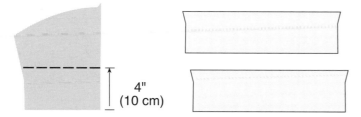

After sewing the sleeve seams, sew the sleeve seams of the facings. Pin the facings to the bottom edges of the sleeves, right sides together, and sew the bottom edges. Overcast the free edges of the facings.

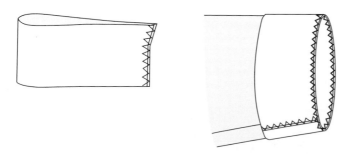

Fold the facing to the wrong side and press. Pin the top edge of the facing to the sleeve. Sew close to the edge of the facing to keep it in place. Roll up the sleeves.

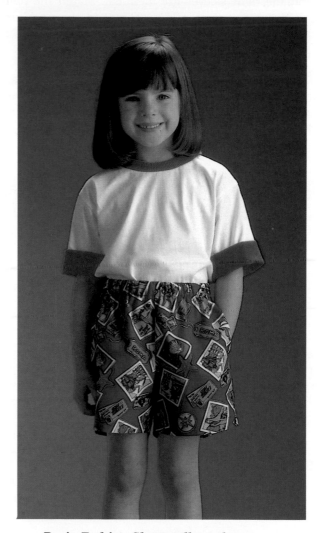

Basic T-shirt, Short roll-up sleeves, Shorts, Pockets in side seams.

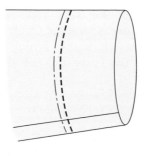

WAISTBAND

Instead of hemming a T-shirt on the bottom edge, you can add a ribbing waistband. When you are cutting out the front and the back, follow the bottom line marked **dress bodice.** For the waistband, use Master pattern piece 6 and cut it from ribbing. Make sure to follow the arrows for the grain and the stretch of the ribbing and place the pattern piece on the fold of the ribbing.

Sew the side seam of the waistband, right sides together, using a straight stitch. Press the seam open. Fold the waistband double lengthwise, with the wrong sides and the raw edges together. Divide the waistband and the bottom of the shirt into fourths with pins.

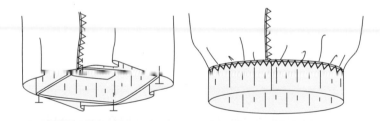

Pin the waistband to the bottom of the shirt with the right sides and the raw edges together. Place the seam on the waistband at one side seam and match the remaining pins. Sew on the waistband, stretching it to fit the bottom edge of the T-shirt.

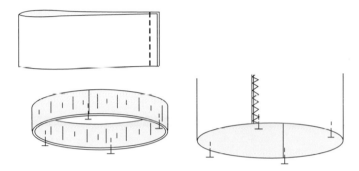

Basic T-shirt, Waistband, Cuffs.

SELF FABRIC NECKBAND, WAISTBAND AND CUFFS

If you are making a shirt from interlock fabric which has at least 25% stretch, you can obtain a nice variation by using the same fabric for the neckband, waistband and the cuffs as you used for the body of the T-shirt. The pattern pieces for the neckband, waistband and the cuffs need to be adjusted. Add to the pattern pieces the following amount: Neckband – ¾" (2 cm), Waistband – 1" (2.5 cm), Cuffs – ½" (1.3 cm). Sew the self fabric bands, using the same procedures as for the ribbing bands.

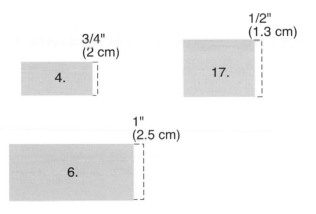

SIDE HEMLINE SLITS

Many children like slits on the sides of their T-shirts. Slits can be as long as you want them to be, however, these instructions are for 3" (7 cm) slits. At the side seams of the front and the back, add for the facings as follows: Mark 4¼" (11 cm) above the bottom edge and add ¾" (2 cm) at the side to this mark.

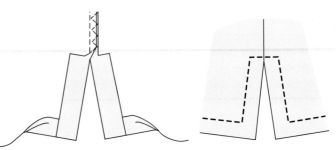

Sew the T-shirt, following the basic instructions, when sewing the side seams, start 4" (10 cm) above the bottom edge and sew to the bottom edge of the sleeve.

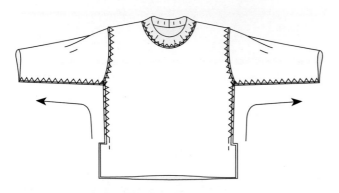

To finish the bottom of the slit, fold 1" (2.5 cm) for the facing to the right side and sew a seam 1" (2.5 cm) from the bottom edge. Trim the hem on the facing. Turn the facing and the hem to the inside and press. Sew close to the edges of the facings and the hem.

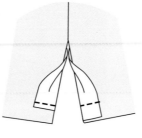

POCKET

To add a pocket to the T-shirt, use Master pattern piece 5. We recommend sewing on the pocket before you sew the shirt together. You may wish to use the same fabric as the shirt or a contrasting fabric can be used.

Cut out the pocket. Stabilize the pocket facing, cut a piece of fusible interfacing the size of the pocket facing and fuse to the wrong side. Overcast the raw edge of the pocket facing.

Fold the facing on the fold line to the right side and sew each side the width of the facing. Turn the facing to the wrong side. Fold under the raw edges of the pocket ¼" (6 mm) and press. Sew close to the edge of the facing.

The placement of the pocket is marked on Master pattern piece 1. The most common position for a pocket is on the left side of the shirt. However, you can place it anywhere you prefer. Place the top edge of the pocket on the pocket placement line. Topstitch around the pocket, leaving the top edge open. Reinforce the top corners of the pocket by sewing a small triangle as illustrated.

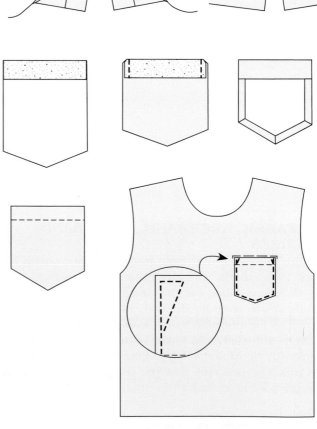

SHIRT WITH PLACKET AND COLLAR

This very popular type of shirt for children is usually referred to as a tennis or polo shirt. It has a front placket and a collar. The collar can be made from self fabric, contrasting fabric - both woven and knit fabric, or you can use a purchased ribbed collar with finished edges.

Use Master pattern pieces:
1. T-shirt Front
2. T-shirt Back
3. T-shirt Sleeve
7. T-shirt Placket
9. T-shirt Upper Collar
10. T-shirt Under Collar

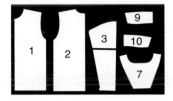

Trace the pattern pieces. On the front and the back, follow **neckline B**. Cut out the shirt, following the layout. If using contrasting fabric for the placket and collar, eliminate pattern pieces 7, 9 and 10. Cut out pattern pieces 7, 9 and 10 from contrasting fabric, no layout given.

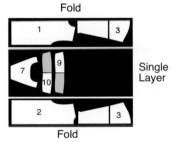

The pattern and the instructions are given for a placket which overlaps left over right, this is for boys. If you want to change to right over left for girls, change the placket and the marking for the slit to the opposite side and reverse all instructions for the left and the right sides.

Fuse interfacing to the wrong side of the placket. Transfer the markings for the slit and the fold line to the interfaced side of the placket. On the front, mark center front and the slit to the right front.

Pin the placket to the front, right sides together, matching the markings for the slit. Using a straight stitch, sew ⅛" (2 mm) from the line marked, sew to a point at the bottom of the slit, pivot, and sew the other side. Cut the slit from the neckline to ⅛" (2 mm) above the point of stitching.

On the right front, fold the facing on the fold line to the inside and press to form the tab. On the left front, fold the facing to the inside on the seam line and press. Overlap the left front over the right front and pin through all layers. At the bottom of the slit, sew a ¼" (6 mm) by 1" (2.5 cm) rectangle through all layers.

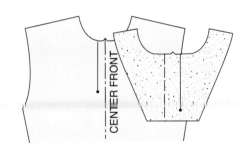

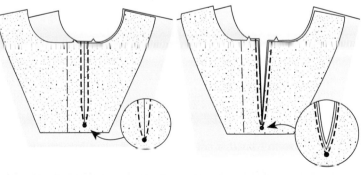

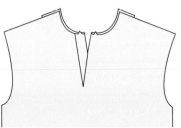

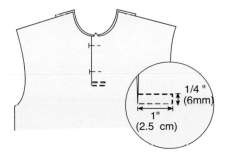

Sew the shoulder seams.

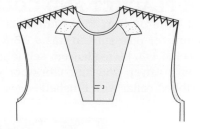

Fuse interfacing to the wrong side of the upper collar. Pin the upper collar to the under collar, right sides together and sew the outside edges, leaving the neckline open. Trim the corners, turn the collar right side out and press.

Pin the collar to the right side of the neckline with the upper collar facing up. Match the center back, the notches to the shoulder seams, and the ends of the collar to the notches for the center front (on the left front, center front is at the notch on the shirt, on the right front, at the notch on the placket). Sew on the collar.

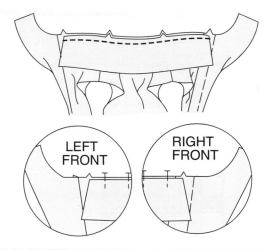

On the left front, fold the facing on seam line to the right side over the collar and pin. On the right front, fold the facing on the fold line to the right side over the collar (the facings extend ¼" (6 mm) past the shoulder seams) and pin. Sew the facings through all layers.

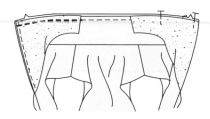

Turn the facings to the inside and press. Attach the ends of the facings to the shoulder seams.

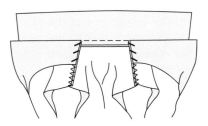

NECKLINE BINDING

If you wish to cover the raw edges on the back neckline, use Master pattern piece 11 - Back neckline binding.

After sewing on the collar and the facing, pin the binding to the back neckline, right sides together, over the collar, matching the center back and the ends of the binding extending ½" (1.3 cm) past the edges of the facings. Sew the binding in the previous seam.

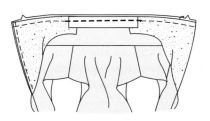

Turn the facings to the inside. Fold under the raw edge of the binding and pin over the seam. Sew close to the edge of the binding. Attach the ends of the facings to the shoulder seams.

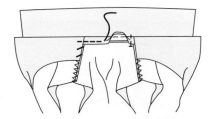

Mark two buttonholes on the left front. The most common position of the buttonholes is to have the top buttonhole horizontal and the other vertical. Mark the top buttonhole ½" (1.3 cm) below the neckline and ½" (1.3 cm) from the edge. Mark the other buttonhole 2" (5 cm) above the bottom of the slit and ⅝" (1.5 cm) from the edge. Make the buttonholes and sew on the buttons to match the buttonholes. Instead of using buttons and buttonholes, you may prefer to use snaps. Finish the shirt as previously described.

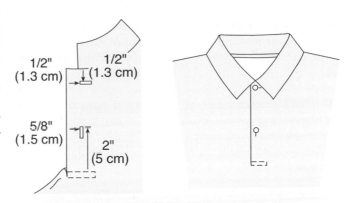

RIBBED COLLAR

Purchased ribbed collars give a ready-to-wear look to a shirt. Collars are available in solid colors, with borders, and with a variety of edge finishes. Collars are available in a variety of sizes, if possible purchase children's sizes, however, you can use the adult size and the collar can be trimmed.

If you are using a ribbed collar, eliminate Master pattern pieces 9 and 10 for the collar. The collar will look the best, if it is a little shorter than the neckline and is stretched across the back neckline to fit.

The following is the approximate measurement for the collar:

XS	S	M	L	XL
11¾"	12"	12½"	12¾"	13"
30 cm	31 cm	32 cm	33 cm	34 cm

If the collar is too long, trim the same amount on both ends, cutting very carefully following the rib. Apply liquid fray preventer to the ends.

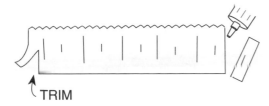

TRIM

Another way to shorten the collar is to make a center back seam. After sewing the seam, press the seam open and attach the seam allowances to the collar with hand stitches. Or you can trim the ends of the collar, fold the ends to the wrong side and sew in place with hand stitches.

The width of the collar should be approximately 2½" - 3" (6 cm - 8 cm); trim if necessary. Trim the collar at the neckline edge as illustrated. Sew on the collar, using the same procedures as for a regular collar.

Shirt with placket and collar, Ribbed collar, Pocket, Side hemline slits, Basic shorts, Pockets in side seams.

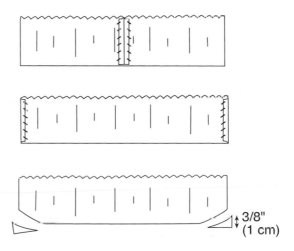

3/8"
(1 cm)

FRONT PLACKET AND FACED NECKLINE

When making a front placket without a collar, follow the instructions for making SHIRT WITH PLACKET AND COLLAR to the point where you have sewn the shoulder seams.

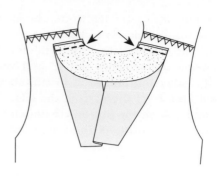

For the back neckline facing, use Master pattern piece 8. Fuse interfacing to the wrong side of the back neckline facing. Sew the back facing to the front facings at the shoulder seams, using a straight stitch and press the seams open.

Pin the facing to the neckline, right sides together; on the left front, fold the facing on the seam line, on the right front, fold the facing on the fold line, matching the center back and the shoulder seams. Sew on the facing. If you wish to make the neck opening wider, sew using a ⅝" (1.5 cm) seam allowance. After you have sewn the seam, trim the seam allowance to ¼" (6 mm) and clip.

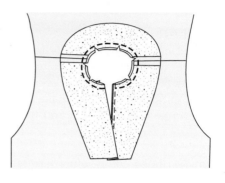

Under stitch the seam allowance to the facing; start and stop the stitching as close as possible to the front edges. Fold the facing to the inside and press. Attach the facings to the shoulder seams with hand stitches or "stitch in the ditch" on the shoulder seams to keep the facing in place. Make the buttonholes and sew on buttons as previously described.

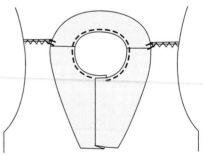

SHIRT WITH COLLAR AND FRONT ZIPPER

Another variation for a front opening can be obtained with an exposed zipper at the center front.
Use Master pattern pieces :
1. T-shirt Front
2. T-shirt Back
3. T-shirt Sleeve
12. T-shirt Collar

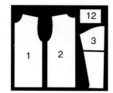

Trace the pattern pieces and follow **neckline B** on the front and the back. Cut out the pattern pieces, following the layouts.

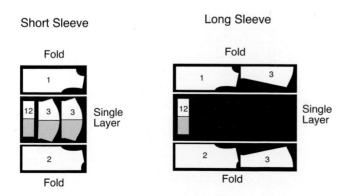

Use a 7" (18 cm) zipper for sizes XS, S, and M, and a 9" (22 cm) for sizes L and XL.

Cut a strip of fusible interfacing ½" (1.3 cm) wide and draw a line in the center of the strip (on the side without the glue). Mark 5½" (14 cm) for sizes XS, S and M and 7¼" (17.5 cm) for sizes L and XL. Trim the interfacing ½" (1.3 cm) below the slit marked.

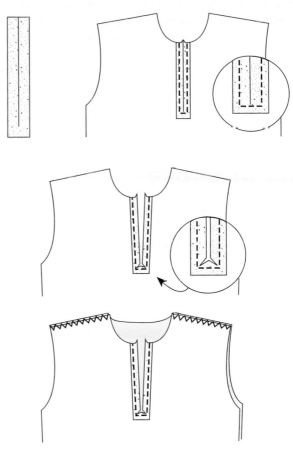

On the wrong side of the front, mark the center front with basting stitches or a water soluble pen. Fuse the interfacing strip to the wrong side of the front, matching the marked line to the center front. Stay stitch ⅛" (2 mm) on each side of the line marked and across the bottom of the marked line.

Cut a slit from the neckline to ¼" (6 mm) above the bottom of the stitching and clip to each corner of the stitching.

Sew the front to the back, right sides together, at the shoulder seams.

Fold the collar on the fold line, wrong sides together, and press. Pin one edge of the collar to the neckline, right sides together, matching the center back, the notches to the shoulder seams and the ends of the collar to the edges of the front. Sew on the collar. Press the seam allowance toward the collar.

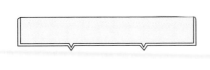

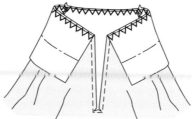

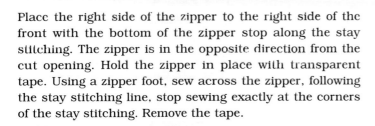

Place the right side of the zipper to the right side of the front with the bottom of the zipper stop along the stay stitching. The zipper is in the opposite direction from the cut opening. Hold the zipper in place with transparent tape. Using a zipper foot, sew across the zipper, following the stay stitching line, stop sewing exactly at the corners of the stay stitching. Remove the tape.

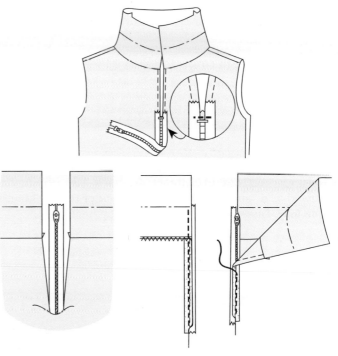

Fold the zipper toward the neckline. Pin the right side of the front to the right side of the zipper with the zipper pull at the fold line on the collar, placing the stay stitching close to the zipper teeth. Sew the zipper to the front along the stay stitching, using a zipper foot. Repeat for the other side.

At the top of the zipper, fold the zipper tape down toward the center front and pin. Fold the extending collar on the fold line to the right side over the zipper. Sew the width of the collar in the same stitching line as for inserting the zipper.

Turn the collar right side out. Pin the collar to the neckline over the seam. On the outside, "stitch in the ditch" to secure the collar on the inside. Topstitch around the zipper ¼" (6 mm) from the edge. Continue sewing the shirt as previously described.

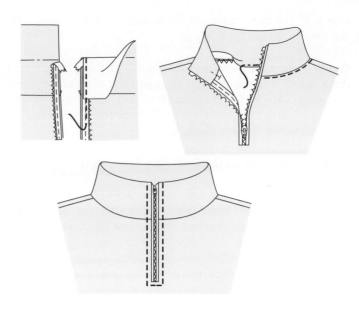

SHIRT WITH YOKE

A yoke can be added to the front or to both the front and the back. This gives you an opportunity to be creative, you can use a striped fabric for the body and a solid color for the yoke, or for the yoke and the sleeves. You can pick a color from the stripes and use this color for the neckband and the cuffs or use different color buttons to match the stripes.

Use Master pattern pieces:
1. T-shirt Front
2. T-shirt Back
3. T-shirt Sleeve
23. Sweatshirt Overlapped neckband

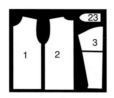

Trace the pattern pieces. On the front and the back, follow **neckline A** when tracing the pattern pieces.

To make the front yoke pattern piece, measure 1½" (4 cm) above the bottom of the armhole, and draw a line perpendicular to the center front. Cut the pattern apart on this line and add ¼" (6 mm) seam allowance to both the yoke and the lower front.

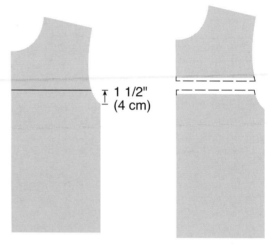

1 1/2"
(4 cm)

At the center front of the yoke pattern piece, add 2" (5 cm), this will be for the overlap and the front facing.

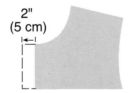

2"
(5 cm)

Adjust the neckband, Master pattern piece 23. Trim the pattern piece ¾" (2 cm) at the center back. Use ribbing for the neckband and place the center back of the neckband on the fold. Disregard the notches on the neckband.

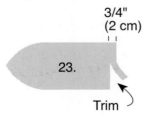

3/4"
(2 cm)

23.

Trim

Cut out the shirt, following the layouts.

Long Sleeve

Fold

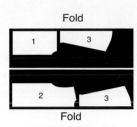

Fold

Short Sleeve

Fold

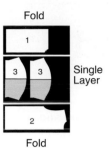

Single Layer

Fold

Contrast Fabric

Selvages

Fold

Stabilize the facings with fusible interfacing, cut two strips 1½" (4 cm) wide and the same length as the yoke. Fuse the interfacing to the wrong side of the facings. Overcast the edges of the facings. Fold 1½" (4 cm) for the facing to the wrong side and press.

Sew the shoulder seams. Fold the neckband lengthwise, wrong sides and raw edges together.

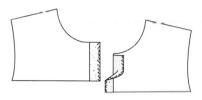

Pin the neckband to the neckline, right sides and raw edges together, matching the center back, and the ends of the neckband at the folding lines (creases) on the yoke. Fold the front facings on the creases to the right side over the neckband. Sew the neckband to the neckline through all layers, stretching the neckband to fit the neckline.

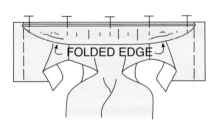

FOLDED EDGE

Turn the facings to the wrong side and press. If you wish, topstitch the neckline close to the seam.

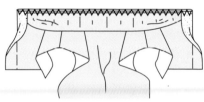

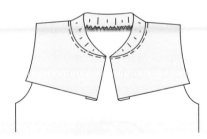

For a boy, overlap the left yoke over the right yoke, matching the center front. For a girl, overlap the right yoke over the left yoke. Sew across the bottom of the yoke to keep it in place.

GIRL   BOY

Sew the yoke to the lower front. Make two vertical button-holes along the center front and sew on buttons to match, or if you prefer, use snaps. Continue sewing the shirt as previously described.

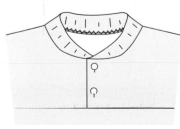

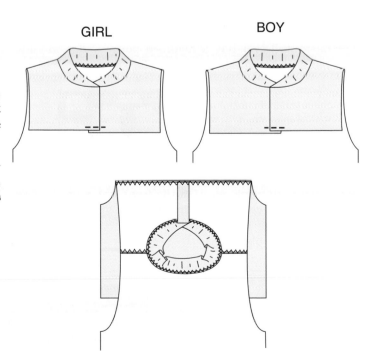

Sweatshirts, Pull-overs and Jackets

The Master pattern includes a pull-over style shirt and a jacket with a button closure on the front. Many variations are included, jackets with zippers, necklines with hood, neckband or collar, bottom edges with waistband or drawstring. You can combine any of the variations to make it just the style you prefer. The shirt has a comfortable relaxed fit and you can use almost any type of fabric, both knit and woven. Use firm knit fabric such as sweatshirt fleece, double knit and heavy single knit, and woven fabrics such as cotton, cotton blends, sheeting, chambray, twill, challis, lightweight denim and windbreaker fabric. This pattern is ideal, because it can be used to make hooded plaid shirts, tunic tops to wear with leggings, bomber jackets, all types of sweatshirts and windbreakers.

The variations you can make are almost endless. After you have made a basic shirt you may want to make variations such as color blocking, with your child's school colors, appliqués or other design changes. The shirts can be made for casual wear as well as for dress up occasions, depending on the fabric. Matched with pants, they become wind suits or jogging suits.

Before making a shirt, be sure to compare the finished length to the length you wish to have and adjust the pattern pieces if necessary. For selecting the size and making adjustments on the pattern, see Pages 7 and 8.

Refer to Pages 11 and 12 for the correct stitches to use for knit or woven fabrics.

PULL-OVER & SWEATSHIRT

The basic pull-over has a hemmed bottom edge, ribbing neckband and long sleeves with cuffs.

Use Master pattern pieces:
13. Sweatshirt Front
14. Sweatshirt Back
15. Sweatshirt Sleeve
16. Sweatshirt Neckband
17. Sweatshirt Cuff

Trace the pattern pieces. On the front, trace on the line for the **pull-over (center front).** Cut out the pattern pieces, following the layout. Cut out the neckband and the cuffs from ribbing.

Fabric 45" (115 cm) or
60" (152 cm) Wide

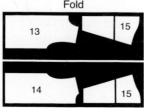

Sweatshirt, Waistband, Purchased appliqué, Shorts, Pockets in side seams.

The finished length of the basic sweatshirt at the center back is as follows:

XS	S	M	L	XL
16½"	17¾"	19"	20½"	22"
42 cm	45 cm	48 cm	52 cm	56 cm

If you are using a stretch fabric, it is necessary to stabilize the shoulder seams. Use non-stretch seam binding or fusible interfacing. Cut two pieces of seam binding the length of the shoulder or cut the interfacing ½" (1.3 cm) wide and the length of the shoulder. Pin the front to the back, right sides together, at the shoulder seams. Place the stabilizing strips to the front shoulders and sew the shoulder seams through all layers. Press the seam allowances toward the back.

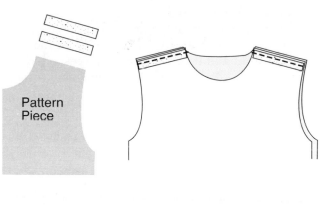

Sew the neckband, sleeves, side seams and the sleeve seams, using the same procedure as for the T-shirt, see Pages 16 and 17.

Sew the sleeve seam of each cuff, right sides together, matching the notches, using a straight stitch and press the seam allowance open. Fold the cuffs double with the wrong sides and the raw edges together. Divide the cuffs and the bottom edges of the sleeves in half with pins.

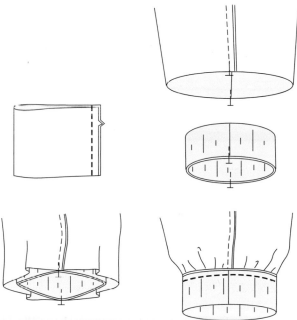

Pin each cuff to the bottom edge of the sleeves, right sides and the raw edges together, matching the seams. Sew on the cuffs, stretching the cuffs to fit the sleeves.

Overcast the bottom edge of the shirt. Fold up a 1" (2.5 cm) hem and press. Sew close to the overcasted edge of the hem.

DRAWSTRING

If you wish to have a drawstring on the bottom of the shirt, mark two ½" (1.3 cm) vertical buttonholes on the front ½" (1.3 cm) from the center front and 1¼" (3.2 cm) above the bottom edge, before sewing the hem. Reinforce the fabric under the position of the buttonholes with a small piece of fusible interfacing. Make the buttonholes. Overcast the bottom edge of the sweatshirt.

Fold 1" (2.5 cm) to the wrong side and sew all the way around close to the edge to form a casing for the drawstring. Insert the drawstring into the casing through the buttonholes. Sew across the casing and the drawstring at the center back, to prevent the drawstring from being pulled out.

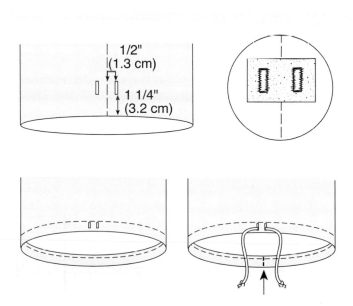

RIBBING WAISTBAND

If you prefer to have a ribbing waistband, take this into consideration before you cut out the shirt. At the bottom of both the front and the back pattern pieces, shorten the pattern 2" (5 cm). For the waistband, use Master pattern piece 6 and add 2" (5 cm) on the fold. Cut the waistband from ribbing, placing it on the fold of the ribbing.

Sew the waistband to the shirt, following instructions on Page 19.

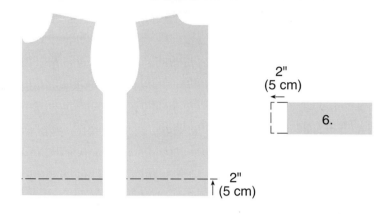

Sweatshirt, Overlapped neckband, Ribbing waistband, Appliqué, Trim, Basic Shorts.

HEMMED SLEEVES

If making short sleeves, overcast the raw edges at the bottom of the sleeves. Fold the hem to the wrong side and sew close to the overcasted edge.

If making long sleeves and you do not wish to have cuffs, you can finish the sleeves with a hem. Before cutting out the garment, add 1¾" (4.5 cm) to the length of the sleeve, which will allow for a ¾" (2 cm) hem, be sure to add an extension to the hem on the sides, as illustrated. Hem the sleeves, using the same procedure as for the short sleeves.

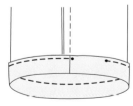

If you wish to insert elastic into the hem, determine the length of the elastic by measuring around the child's wrist and add 1" (2.5 cm). If you do not have the child's measurement, use the following chart and cut two pieces of ⅜" (1 cm) wide elastic.

XS	S	M	L	XL
6"	6¼"	6¾"	7"	7¼"
15 cm	16 cm	17 cm	18 cm	19 cm

When sewing the hem, be sure to leave a 1" (2.5 cm) opening for inserting the elastic. Insert the elastic into the hem, overlap the ends of the elastic ⅜" (1 cm) and sew them together. Finish sewing the casing seam.

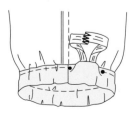
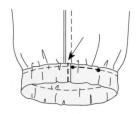
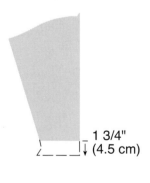

OVERLAPPED NECKBAND

An overlapped neckband gives a nice variation to a sweatshirt. Use Master pattern piece 23 for the neckband and cut from ribbing.

Sew the shoulder seams of the sweatshirt as described previously. Fold the neckband lengthwise, wrong sides and raw edges together. Overlap the left end of the neckband over the right end for boys, and the right over the left for girls, matching the notches for the center front. Sew close to the edge to keep them together.

Pin the neckband to the neckline with the right sides and the raw edges together, matching the notch to the center front, the notches to the shoulder seams and the center back. Sew the neckband, stretching it to fit the neckline. Finish the shirt as previously described.

STAND UP COLLAR WITH DRAWSTRING

If you prefer to have a collar instead of a neckband, use Master pattern piece 21 and cut out the collar from self fabric. When using woven fabric, be sure to cut the collar on the bias. Mark the buttonholes, using the placement and the length marked on the pattern piece. Reinforce the fabric under the position of the buttonholes with a small piece of fusible interfacing. Make the buttonholes.

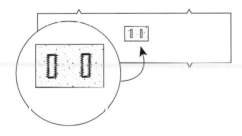

Sew the shoulder seams as previously described. Fold the collar, right sides together, and sew the center back seam. Press the seam allowance open. Fold the collar, wrong sides and raw edges together and press. Topstitch the collar close to the folded edge and sew another seam ⅝" (1.5 cm) from the edge, to make the casing for the drawstring.

Pin the collar to the neckline, with the side with the buttonholes to the right side of the neckline. Match the center back, center front and the notches to the shoulder seams. Sew on the collar. Insert the drawstring through the buttonholes into the casing.

PULL-OVER WITH HOOD

A hood can be used instead of a neckband on the pull-over. The hood has to be made from a knit fabric. If making the shirt from a woven fabric, make the hood from a contrasting knit fabric, such as a single knit or an interlock. The hood can be made with or without a drawstring.

Use Master pattern pieces:
13. Sweatshirt Front
14. Sweatshirt Back
15. Sweatshirt Sleeve
17. Sweatshirt Cuff
19. Sweatshirt Hood

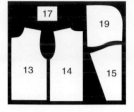

Trace the pattern pieces. On the front, trace on the line for **pull-over (center front).** Cut out the pattern pieces, following the layout. Cut out the cuffs from ribbing.

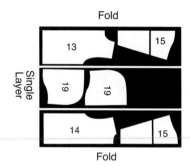

Fabric 60" (152 cm) Wide

Sew the front to the back at the shoulder seams as previously described.

Sew the hoods, right sides together, at the top edge and the center back seam and overcast the front edge.

If you wish to have a drawstring in the hood, buttonholes will be needed. Mark ½" (1.3 cm) vertical buttonholes on each front of the hood 1" (2.5 cm) above the neckline and 1¼" (3.2 cm) from the front edge. Reinforce the fabric under the buttonholes with small pieces of fusible interfacing. Make the buttonholes.

Fold the hood facing on the fold line to the wrong side and press. Sew close to the overcasted edge. Overlap the left side of the hood over the right for boys, overlap the right over the left for girls, matching the notches for the center front. Sew together close to the edges.

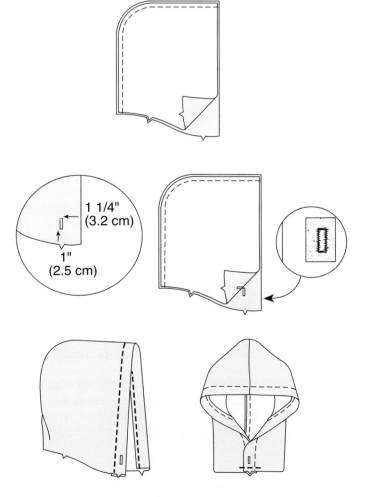

Pin the hood to the neckline, right sides together, matching the seam on the hood to the center back, the notches to the shoulder seams and the notches for the center front. Sew the hood to the neckline. If you are making the hood with a drawstring, insert the drawstring into the hood casing through the buttonholes. Sew through all layers at the center of the hood to keep the drawstring from being pulled out. Finish the shirt as described previously.

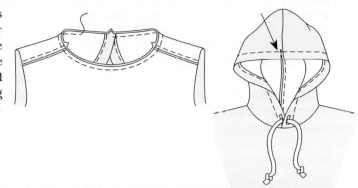

JACKETS & SHIRTS

Jackets and shirts are a must in any wardrobe and they can be made with a button, snap or a zipper closure. Neckline variations include neckband, round neckline with binding, or hood. The bottom edge can be made with waistband, drawstring or hemmed bottom edge.

JACKET WITH BUTTON CLOSURE AND NECKBAND

This jacket has a ribbing neckband and cuffs, front buttonhole and button closure or if you prefer, use snaps. Pockets can be added, see Pages 41-45.

Use Master pattern pieces:
13. Sweatshirt Front
14. Sweatshirt Back
15. Sweatshirt Sleeve
17. Sweatshirt Cuff
23. Sweatshirt Overlapped Neckband

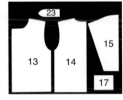

Trace the pattern pieces, on the front, trace on the line for **jacket style.** Cut out the pattern pieces, following the layouts. Cut out the neckband and the cuffs from ribbing.

Fabric 60" (152 cm) Wide

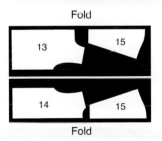

Fabric 45" (115 cm) Wide

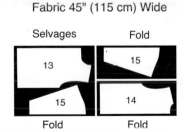

Cut two pieces of fusible interfacing for the front facings and fuse to the wrong side of the front facings. Overcast the raw edges of the facing. Fold the facing on the fold line to the wrong side and press.

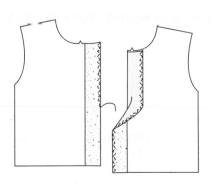

Sew the shoulder seams, sleeves, side seams, sleeve seams and the cuffs as previously described.

Fold the neckband lengthwise, wrong sides and raw edges together. Pin the neckband to the neckline, right sides and raw edges together, matching the center back, the notches to the shoulder seams and the center front. Sew on the neckband, stretching the neckband to fit the neckline.

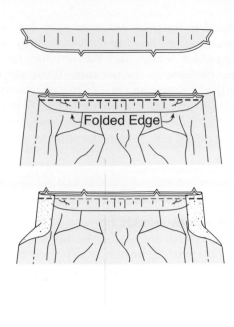

Fold the front facings on the fold lines to the right side over the neckband and pin. Sew the facings in the same seam as for sewing on the neckband. Overcast the raw edges together and if desired, topstitch neckline close to the seam.

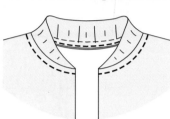

BINDING

If you would like to have a neater finish on the inside, cover the raw edges with a binding. Trace Master pattern piece 20 for the binding. If using a light to medium weight fabric, cut the binding from the same fabric. If using a heavy weight fabric, cut the binding from a lightweight woven fabric. Press the binding double lengthwise, wrong sides together. After you have sewn the neckband, pin the right side of the binding to the neckline over the neckband, matching the center back and the ends of the binding extending ½" (1.3 cm) past the edges of the front facings and all the raw edges together. Sew the binding in the same seam as for sewing on the neckband.

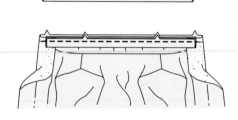

Turn the facing to the wrong side and fold the binding over the seam allowance. Sew close to the edge of the binding and across the front facings.

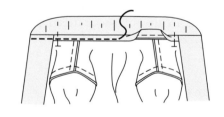

Overcast the bottom edge of the jacket. Fold the front facing to the right side on the fold line, sew across the facing 1" (2.5 cm) above the bottom edge. Trim the facing. Turn the facing to the wrong side and fold up a 1" (2.5 cm) hem and press. Hem the jacket by sewing close to the overcasted edge. If desired, stitch close to the edges of the front facings.

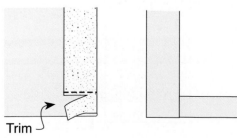

Mark horizontal buttonholes on the front ½" (1.3 cm) from the edge. Mark on the right front for girls and on the left front for boys. Use four buttons for sizes XS-S-M, and five for sizes L and XL. Mark the top buttonhole ⅝" (1.5 cm) below the neckline edge and the remaining the following distance apart: XS - 3¼" (8 cm), S - 3½" (9 cm), M - 4" (10 cm), L - 3½" (9 cm), XL - 3¾" (9.5 cm). Make the buttonholes and sew on the buttons along the center front to match the buttonholes.

If making a shirt and using smaller buttons, additional buttonholes and buttons should be used, be sure to space the buttonholes evenly.

HOOD

This jacket may be made with a hood instead of a neckband. Sew the hood as described for the pull-over with hood on Page 32. Sew the hood to the jacket, using the same method as for sewing on the neckband.

ROUND NECKLINE

If you wish to have a round neckline finished with binding, use Master pattern piece 20 for the binding. Follow the procedures for binding, eliminating all instructions for the neckband.

DRAWSTRING AT THE BOTTOM EDGE

If you wish to have a drawstring, it is necessary to make two buttonholes before you finish the hem. Mark the position for the buttonholes on the bottom edge of each front. Measure 1⅝" (4 cm) from the fold line and 1¼" (3 cm) above the bottom edge. Place a piece of interfacing under the position of the buttonholes and make ½" (1.3 cm) vertical buttonholes.

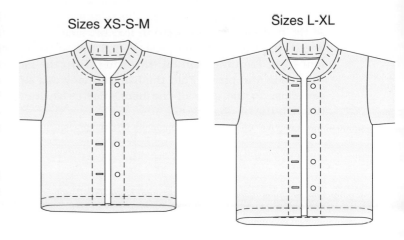

Sizes XS-S-M   Sizes L-XL

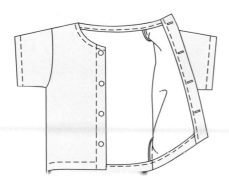

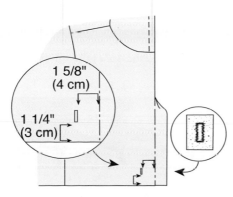

1 5/8" (4 cm)

1 1/4" (3 cm)

Jacket with button closure, Hood, Side hemline slits, Hemmed sleeves, Basic T-shirt.

At the bottom edge of the front, fold the facing on the fold line to the right side and sew 1" (2.5 cm) above the bottom edge. Trim the hem on the facing. Turn the facing to the inside and press. Fold the hem to the wrong side and sew close to the edge of the hem. Insert the drawstring through the buttonholes.

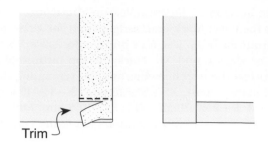

Trim

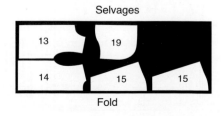

JACKET WITH ZIPPER, HOOD AND RIBBING WAISTBAND

This jacket has a hood, zipper, ribbing cuffs and waistband with self fabric extensions. If you wish to add pockets, see Pages 41-45.

Use Master pattern pieces:
13. Sweatshirt Front
14. Sweatshirt Back
15. Sweatshirt Sleeve
17. Sweatshirt Cuffs
19. Sweatshirt Hood
 6. T-shirt Waistband

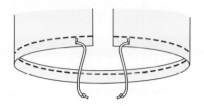

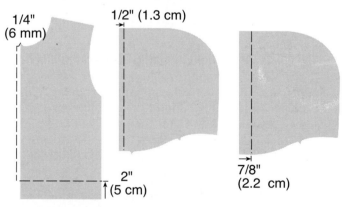

Trace the pattern pieces, on the front, follow the line marked **center front.** On the front pattern piece add ¼" (6 mm) to the center front. Shorten the front and the back pattern pieces 2" (5 cm) at the bottom edge, to allow for the waistband. On the pattern piece for the hood, trim ½" (1.3 cm) from the front edge and mark a new fold line ⅞" (2.2 cm) from the edge. Disregard the center front notch on the hood.

Cut out the pattern pieces, following the layouts. Cut out the waistband and the cuffs from ribbing.

1/4" (6 mm)   1/2" (1.3 cm)

2" (5 cm)   7/8" (2.2 cm)

Fabric 60" (152 cm) Wide

Fold

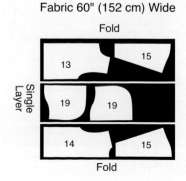

Single Layer

Fold

Fabric 45" (115 cm) Wide

Selvages

Fold

Sew the shoulder seams, sleeves, side seams, sleeve seams, cuffs, center back seam of the hood and make the buttonholes on the hood as previously described.

Cut two pieces of fabric for the waistband extensions 2½" (6 cm) wide and 4¾" (12 cm) long. Pin the fabric extension to each end of the waistband, right sides together, and sew the seams. Press the seam allowances open.

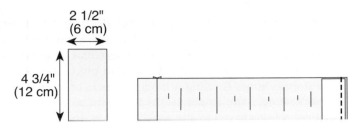

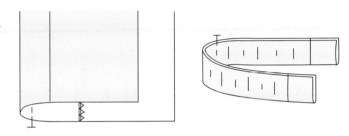

Fold the waistband double lengthwise, with the wrong sides and the raw edges together. Mark the center back of the waistband and the jacket with pins. Pin the waistband to the right side of the bottom edge, matching the pins for the center back and the ends of the waistband even with the front edges. Sew on the waistband, stretching the ribbing waistband to fit the bottom edge.

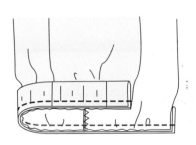 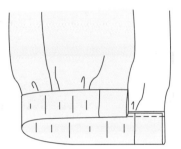

Use a separating zipper, with either a single or a double pull. The length of the zipper depends upon the length of the front of the jacket including the waistband. It is sometimes difficult to purchase the correct length zipper, in that case, purchase a longer zipper than needed, and it will be trimmed after the hood is sewn to the jacket.

Pin the zipper to the front edge, right sides together, place the edge of the zipper tape even with the edge of the front and the bottom of the zipper even with the bottom of the waistband. If using a longer zipper, the zipper will extend above the neckline. Using a zipper foot, sew the zipper ⅜" (1 cm) from the edge. Repeat for the other side. Fold the seam allowance to the wrong side and press. Topstitch ¼" (6 mm) from the seam through the zipper, jacket and the seam allowance.

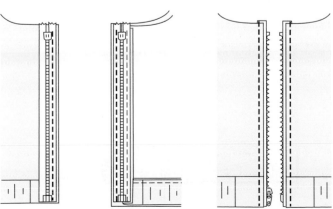

Jacket with zipper, Hood, Ribbing waistband, Welt pockets, Hair scrunchy, Basic shorts.

Pin the hood to the neckline, right sides together, matching the center back, the notches to the shoulder seams, and the fold line on the hood to the edges of the zipper. Fold the hood facing to the inside and pin. Sew the hood to the neckline. If using a longer zipper, be careful when you sew over the zipper teeth; it is best to use the hand wheel to slowly guide the machine over the zipper. Trim the extending zipper, if necessary. Turn the hood facing to the inside. Topstitch the front of the hood close to the edge of the facing.

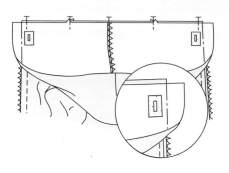
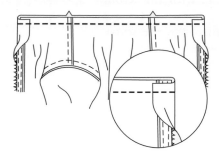
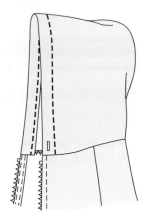

DRAWSTRING AT BOTTOM EDGE

Instead of a waistband at the bottom edge, you can make a casing with a drawstring. When tracing the pattern pieces for the front and the back, be sure to use the bottom line on the Master pattern. The instructions for sewing the zipper are the same as previously described, except the bottom edge of the zipper has to be placed 2" (5 cm) above the bottom edge of the front. After sewing the zipper to the front, topstitch ¼" (6 mm) from the seam and continue to the bottom of the jacket.

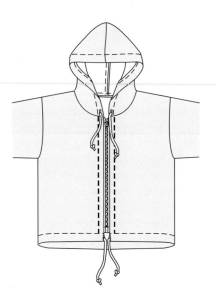

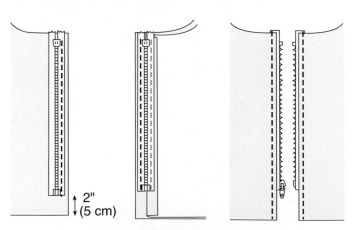

Overcast the bottom edge, fold a 1" (2.5 cm) hem to the wrong side and sew close to the overcasted edge. Insert the drawstring through the openings below the zipper.

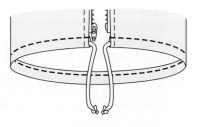

JACKET WITH ZIPPER, NECKBAND AND DRAWSTRING

This jacket has a zipper with a front facing, ribbing neckband and cuffs, and a drawstring at the bottom edge.

Use Master pattern pieces:
13. Sweatshirt Front
14. Sweatshirt Back
15. Sweatshirt Sleeve
17. Sweatshirt Cuff
20. Sweatshirt Neckline Binding
23. Sweatshirt Overlapped Neckband

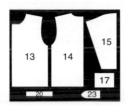

Trace the pattern pieces. On the front, trace on the line marked **center front** and add ¼" (6 mm) to the center front. Shorten the neckband, Master pattern piece 23, ⅝" (1.5 cm) on the front part of the neckband, see illustration. Trim the neckline binding, Master pattern piece 20, at the notches for the shoulders.

The front edge will have a front facing and a pattern piece is not included. To make the front facing pattern piece, trace the adjusted front 3" (7.5 cm) from the front edge and trace to the shoulder as illustrated.

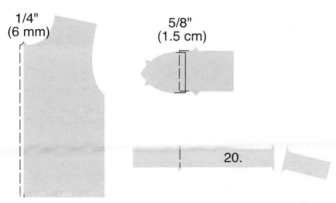

Cut out the jacket, following the layouts. Cut out the neckband and the cuffs from ribbing.

Sew the shoulder seams, the sleeves to the jacket, the side seams, the sleeve seams and the cuffs as described previously.

Fabric 60" (152 cm) Wide

Fabric 45" (115 cm) Wide

Pin the zipper to the front, right sides together, with the bottom of the zipper 2" (5 cm) above the bottom edge and the zipper tape even with the raw edge of the front. At the neckline, fold the zipper toward the outside **½" (1.3 cm) below** the neckline. Sew the zipper to the front ⅜" (1 cm) from the edge of the zipper tape and across the zipper teeth, see illustration. Repeat for the other side.

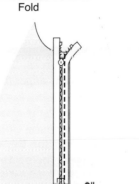

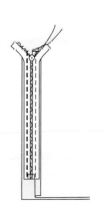

39

Pin the front facing to the jacket at the front edge, right sides together, with the zipper in between. Sew from the neckline to the **bottom of the zipper;** do not sew to the bottom edge of the jacket as an opening will be needed for the drawstring.

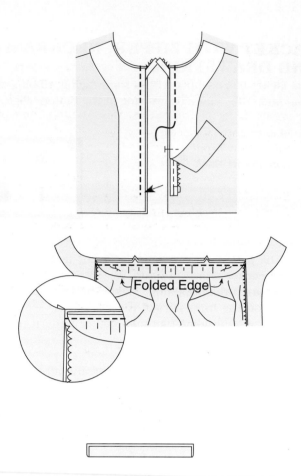

Fold the neckband lengthwise, wrong sides and raw edges together. Disregard the notches for the center front. Pin the neckband to the neckline, right sides and raw edges together, matching the center back, the notches to the shoulder seams and with the ends of the neckband at the seam for the zipper. Sew the neckband, stretching the neckband to fit; do not catch the zipper tape with your stitches.

Fold the front facing to the right side over the neckband and pin; facings extend ¼" (6 mm) past the shoulder seams. Fold the binding double, wrong sides and raw edges together. Pin the right side of the binding to the back neckline over the neckband, matching the center back and the ends of the binding, overlapping the facings ¼" (6 mm). Sew the facing and the binding in the same seam as for sewing on the neckband. Trim the extending zipper even with the seam allowance. Turn the facing to the inside. Fold the binding over the seam allowance and stitch close to the edge of the binding. Attach the facings to the shoulder seams.

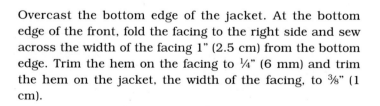

Overcast the bottom edge of the jacket. At the bottom edge of the front, fold the facing to the right side and sew across the width of the facing 1" (2.5 cm) from the bottom edge. Trim the hem on the facing to ¼" (6 mm) and trim the hem on the jacket, the width of the facing, to ⅜" (1 cm).

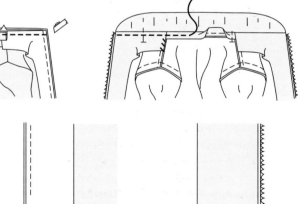

Turn the facing to the inside and press. Tuck in the raw edges of the opening at the bottom edge. Topstitch close to the bottom edge the width of the facing. Fold up a 1" (2.5 cm) hem to the wrong side and sew close to the over-casted edge. Topstitch the front edges ¼" (6 mm) from the zipper seam, stopping at the seam for the casing. Insert the drawstring through the opening below the zipper.

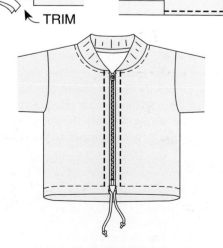

POCKETS

Pockets can be added to any pull-over shirt or jacket and pockets should always be sewn to the garment before the side seams are sewn. Four different pockets are included: kangaroo pocket, side pockets, welt pockets, and patch pocket with a zipper.

KANGAROO POCKET

Trace Master pattern piece 18 for the pocket. This pocket can be placed on the front of a pull-over with a hem or a drawstring at the bottom edge. If making a shirt with waistband, trim 1½" (4 cm) off the bottom edge of the pocket.

1 1/2"
↑ (4 cm)

At the pocket opening, fold ¾" (2 cm) to the wrong side and press. Fold under the raw edge ¼" (6 mm) and press. Sew close to the edge. At the sides of the pocket, press the seam allowances to the wrong side.

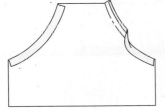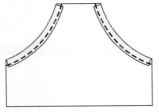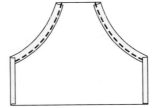

To mark the position of the pocket, place the pocket on the front with the right sides up, and the raw edges together at the bottom edge, matching the center front of the pocket to the center front of the shirt. Mark the top edge of the pocket with pins and mark the pocket placement **½" (1.3 cm) below the pins.**

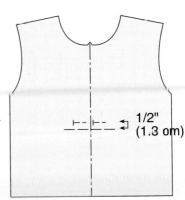

1/2"
(1.3 om)

Place the top raw edge of the pocket on the placement line, right sides together; the bottom edge of the pocket is now close to the neckline. Sew the top of the pocket to the front ¼" (6 mm) from the edge. Fold the pocket down and pin to the bottom edge of the front. Topstitch the sides of the pocket close to the edge and reinforce the pocket opening as illustrated. Sew the bottom of the pocket to the front.

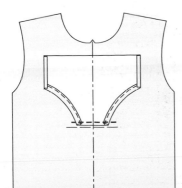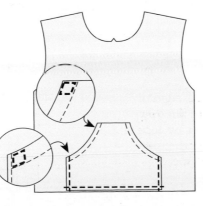

If you are using a kangaroo pocket on a jacket with a zipper, add ½" (1.3 cm) to the width of the pocket pattern piece along the center front and cut two. Apply the pocket to each front, using the same procedures.

1/2"
(1.3 cm)

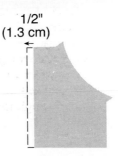

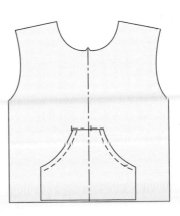

SIDE POCKETS

Trace Master pattern piece 22 for the pocket. The side pocket can be placed on a pull-over shirt or a jacket with a hemmed bottom edge. If making the side pockets on a shirt with waistband, the placement of the pockets has to be adjusted. Pocket can be made with a rounded or square front bottom edge.

Cut out two pockets. Cut two pieces of fusible interfacing for the pocket facings and fuse to the wrong side of the pocket facings.

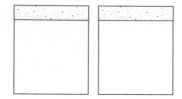

Rounded pocket
Fold the pocket facing on the·fold line to the right side and sew the **front edge** of the pocket the width of the facing, continue sewing the pocket on the seam line to the side seam. Sew gathering stitches in the middle of the seam allowance on the curved front edge of the pocket. Turn the facing to the inside. Fold under the seam allowance on the front and the bottom edge of the pocket along the stitching; pull up the gathering stitches to ease the seam allowance and press. Sew close to the edge of the facing.

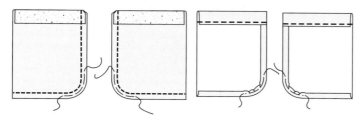

Jacket with button closure, Hood, Side pockets, Basic pants, Basic T-shirt.

Square pocket
Fold the pocket facing on the fold line to the right side and sew the **front edge** of the pocket the width of the facing. Trim the corners. Turn the facing to the inside and press. Fold under the seam allowance on the front and the bottom edge and press. Sew close to the edge of the facing.

Place the pocket on each front with the bottom edge of the pocket 2" (5 cm) above the bottom edge and the raw edges even at the side seam. Sew on the pocket by topstitching close to the edges and sew pocket to the side seam to hold the pocket in place.

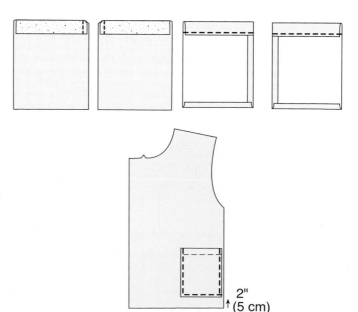

2"
(5 cm)

WELT POCKETS

Trace Master pattern piece 24. Welt pockets can be added to a pull-over shirt or a jacket with any hem finish. Cut two pockets from self fabric and cut the interfacing as marked on the pattern piece. Fuse the interfacing to the wrong side of the pockets at the placement marked on the pattern. Transfer the stitching lines for the welt to the interfaced side of the pockets and to the fronts.

Jacket with zipper and hood, Drawstring at bottom edge, Welt pockets, Color blocking Design B, Basic pants.

Pin the pocket to the front, with the notched edge of the pocket toward the bottom edge, matching the lines on the pocket to the placement on the front. Sew all the way around the rectangle.

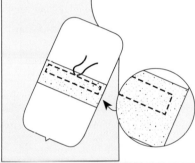

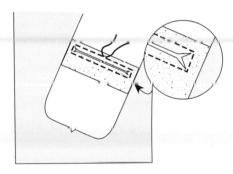

Cut a slit in the middle of the stitching lines, stopping ½" (1.3 cm) from the ends and clip to each corner of the stitching.

Turn the pocket piece to the inside. Press the lower seam allowance open and press the top seam allowance up.

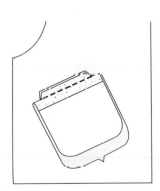

To make the welt, fold the bottom of the pocket, wrong sides together, and pin to cover the opening. Press and baste with hand stitches if desired.

Secure the welt by topstitching on the front close to the seam and be sure not to catch the upper part of the pocket.

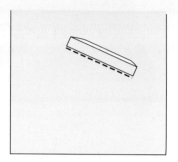

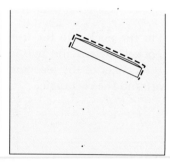

On the inside, fold the pocket, right sides together, and sew the sides and the bottom edge. Overcast the raw edges together. Topstitch the sides and the top edge of the pocket close to the seams.

PATCH POCKET WITH ZIPPER

Patch pocket with zipper can be added to any pull-over style shirt. A pattern piece is not included and the pocket can be made any size. If using heavyweight fabric, use a lining fabric for the facing. To make a pocket 8½" x 6½" (20 cm x 16.5 cm), and using a 7" (18 cm) zipper, cut a piece of fabric 9" x 7" (23 cm x 18 cm). Cut a piece of fabric for the facing 9" x 3" (23 cm x 8 cm). Cut a piece of fusible interfacing for the facing and fuse to the wrong side. Mark a ⅜" (1 cm) rectangle on the facing 1¼" (3 cm) below the top edge and the ends of the rectangle 1" (2.5 cm) from the edges.

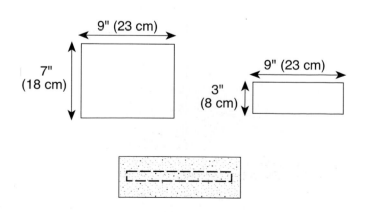

Pull-over with hood, Drawstring, Patch pocket with zipper, Basic pants.

Pin the facing to the pocket, right sides together, with the top edges even and sew the marked rectangle. Cut a slit in the middle of the rectangle, stopping ½" (1.3 cm) from the ends and clip to each corner. Turn the facing to the wrong side and press, rolling the seam slightly to the facing side.

Center the zipper underneath the opening with the zipper teeth exposed. Baste or tape in place. Topstitch around the zipper close to the edge. Trim the facing close to the zipper tape on the inside and overcast together. Press the seam allowance around the pocket to the wrong side. Pin the pocket to the front at position desired and topstitch all around the pocket.

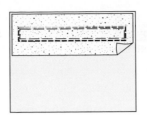 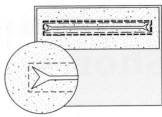

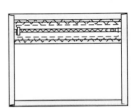

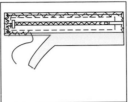

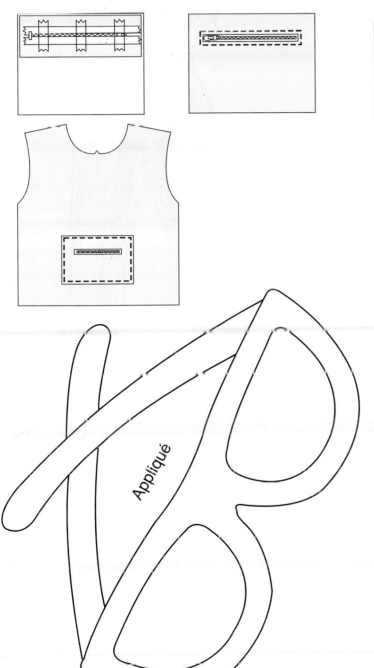

Pull-over with hood, Drawstring, Basic pants, Pockets in side seams.

Pants and Shorts

Pants and shorts are very easy to make and most children do not seem to have enough of them. The Master pattern includes pull-on type pants and shorts with elastic in a casing at the waist and they can be made with or without pockets. The pants can be made in woven or firm knit fabrics. Use woven fabrics such as cotton, cotton types, linen types, gabardine, sheeting, windbreaker fabrics and twill or knit fabrics such as sweatshirt fleece, French terry, double knits and heavy single knit. If you are using a fabric with more stretch, such as stretch velour or interlock, the pants will have a looser fit.

If you would like a matching sweatsuit or a windsuit, use the same fabric as you used for the shirt or jacket. Coordinate an outfit by using the pants fabric for an appliqué or for color blocking on the shirt.

For choosing the size and making adjustments, see Pages 7 and 8. The finished length of the pants and shorts at the outside leg seam is listed below. Determine if the length needs adjusting by comparing the child's measurements to those listed. Measure the child at the outside leg or measure a pair of pants that fit. If length needs adjusting, lengthen or shorten both the front and the back, using the shorten and lengthen line given on the pattern.

The finished length at the outside leg seam is as follows:
PANTS

XS	S	M	L	XL
22¾"	25¾"	28¾"	31¾"	34 ¾"
57 cm	65 cm	73 cm	81 cm	88 cm

SHORTS

11"	11¾"	12½"	13½"	14½"
28 cm	29.5 cm	31.5 cm	34 cm	36.5 cm

The finished width at the bottom edge of the pants is as follows:

XS	S	M	L	XL
10½"	11"	11½"	12"	12½"
27 cm	28 cm	29 cm	31 cm	32 cm

If your child has a personal preference for either wider or narrower legs, the leg width can easily be changed. You have to remember, that changes have to be made on both the inside and the outside leg seams on both the front and the back pattern pieces.

Determine how much wider or narrower you want the leg to be. Divide this measurement into four. On the bottom of the leg on the front and the back, mark inside the original pattern line to decrease the width. To increase the width, mark outside the original pattern line. Now draw a line from the bottom of the leg to the line for shorts marked on the Master pattern.

BASIC PANTS OR SHORTS
WITHOUT POCKETS

Use Master pattern pieces:
25. Pants Front
26. Pants Back

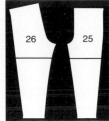

The Master Pattern includes a 1"
(2.5 cm) hem at the bottom of the
pants and the shorts and 1⅜" (3.5
cm) is allowed for the casing at the
waist.

Trace the pattern pieces and make any necessary adjustment on the pattern. Cut out the pants or the shorts, following the layouts.

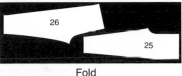

<table>
<tr><td>Pants
Fabric 45" (115 cm) Wide
Sizes: XS-S-M</td><td>Pants
Fabric 45" (115 cm) Wide
Sizes: L-XL</td></tr>
</table>

Pants or Shorts
Fabric 60"
(152 cm) Wide
All Sizes

Shorts
Fabric 45" (115 cm) Wide
Sizes: XS-S-M-L

Shorts
Fabric 45" (115 cm) Wide
Size: XL

Place the back and the front, right sides together, and
sew the outside leg seam. Press the seam allowance
toward the back. Sew the inside leg seams, right sides
together. Press the seam allowance toward the front.

Turn one leg right side out. Place this leg inside the other
leg, right sides together. Pin the center front and the center back seams, matching the inside leg seams and the
waist edges. Sew from the front waist to the back waist.

Overcast the waist and fold 1⅜" (3.5 cm) to the wrong
side for the casing and press.

Cut a piece of 1" (2.5 cm) wide elastic the
following length:

XS	S	M	L	XL
20"	21"	22"	22½"	23½"
51 cm	53 cm	56 cm	58 cm	60 cm

Overlap the ends of the elastic ⅜" (1 cm) and sew them
together. Place the elastic inside the casing and using a
zipper foot, sew all the way around the waist. Sew as
close as possible to the elastic, without catching the elastic with the stitches. Sew without stretching the elastic;
when needed, stop and pull the elastic from the sewn casing, to keep the fabric and the elastic flat where you are
sewing. Sew as far as you can, pull the elastic and continue until the entire casing seam is completed.

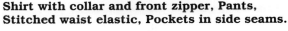

Shirt with collar and front zipper, Pants,
Stitched waist elastic, Pockets in side seams.

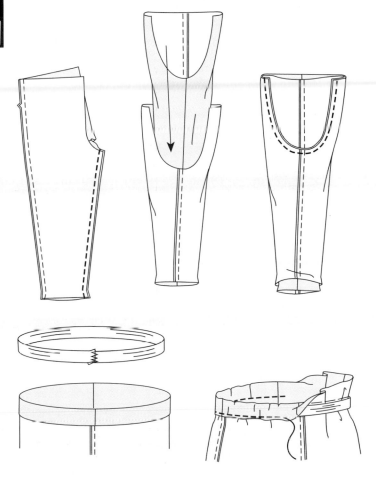

Distribute the gathers evenly by stretching the elastic repeatedly. To keep the elastic from rolling, sew across the width of the elastic, at the outside leg seams, the center front and the center back.

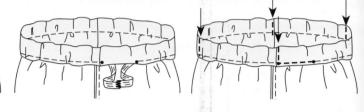

Another method of finishing the waist is to sew the casing first, leaving a 1" (2.5 cm) opening for inserting the elastic. Hook a safety pin to one end of the elastic and thread into the casing through the opening. Overlap the ends of the elastic and sew them together. Finish sewing the casing seam. Sew across the width of the elastic as described previously.

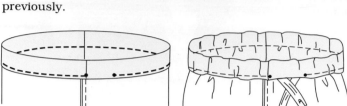

At the bottom edge of the leg, fold a 1" (2.5 cm) hem to the wrong side and press. Sew close to the edge.

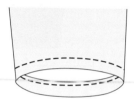

LEG ELASTIC

If you prefer to have elastic at the bottom of the legs, fold ¾" (2 cm) to the wrong side and stitch close to the edge, leaving an opening for inserting the elastic.

Cut two pieces of ½" (1.3 cm) wide elastic the following length:

XS	S	M	L	XL
6¾"	7"	7½"	7¾"	8"
17 cm	18 cm	19 cm	20 cm	21 cm

Insert the elastic into the casing. Overlap the ends of the elastic and sew them together. Finish sewing the casing seam. To keep the elastic from rolling, sew across the width of the elastic at the inside and the outside leg seams.

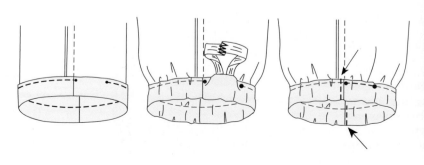

Jacket with zipper, neckband and drawstring. Color blocked Design F. Pants, Pockets in side seams, Leg elastic.

LEG CUFFS

If you are making sweatpants or pajamas it is a good idea to add cuffs to the bottom of the legs. The pattern pieces for the front and the back need to be shortened to allow for the cuff. Shorten the front and the back pattern pieces 2" (5 cm) at the bottom edge. Use Master pattern piece 17 for the cuffs and add 1" (2.5 cm) to the notched edge of the pattern piece.

Cut out the cuffs from ribbing. Sew the ends of each cuff, right sides together, matching the notches. Use a straight stitch and press the seam open. Fold the cuff double, wrong sides and the raw edges together. Divide the cuff and the bottom edge of the leg in half with pins. Pin the cuff to the bottom edge of the leg opening, right sides and raw edges together, matching the pins and the seam on the cuff to the inside leg seam. Sew on the cuff, stretching the cuff to fit the leg opening.

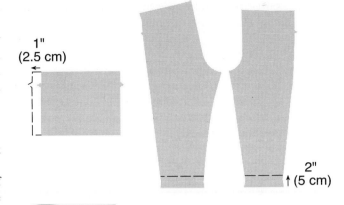

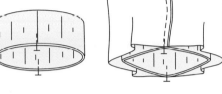

CONTRASTING ROLL-UP CUFFS

You may want to finish the bottom of the legs with roll-up cuffs from contrasting fabric. Use a light to medium weight woven fabric for the cuffs. Lengthen the pattern pieces for the pants 2" (5 cm), using the shorten and the lengthen line on the pattern. Eliminate the extensions for the hem as illustrated.

A Master pattern is not included for the cuffs. To make the pattern pieces for the cuffs, trace the bottom of the legs and draw a line across the pattern 4" (10 cm) above the bottom edge. Cut the cuffs from a contrasting fabric, cutting two of each pattern piece.

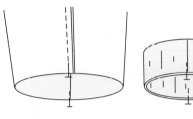

Sew the pants as previously described. Pin the front and the back leg cuffs, right sides together, and sew the inside and the outside leg seams. Overcast the top edge of the cuffs.

Pin the leg cuffs, to the bottom edges of the legs, right sides together, matching the seams and sew the bottom edges. Fold the cuffs to the inside and press. Pin the top edges of the cuffs to the pants. Sew close to the edges of the cuffs, to keep in place, by machine or by hand. Fold up the cuffs.

 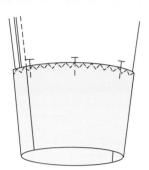

POCKETS IN SIDE SEAMS

Adding pockets to either shorts or pants is very easy. You have to sew the pockets to the side seams before you sew anything else on the pants. Trace Master pattern piece 27 for the pocket and cut four.

Pin one pocket to the front at the outside leg seam, right sides together, matching the notches. Sew on the pocket, using a ¼" (6 mm) seam allowance. Repeat for the other front and the backs. Fold the pockets out from the pants and press.

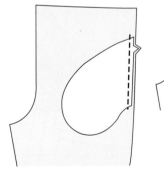

Pin the front and the back, right sides together, at the outside leg seams. Pin the pockets, right sides together, and sew from the bottom edge of the leg, around the pocket, to the waist. Press the pockets toward the front. Continue sewing the pants as previously described.

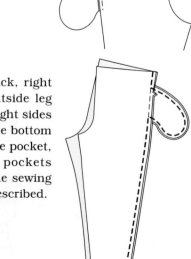

Sweatshirt, Overlapped neckband, Drawstring at the bottom edge, Basic shorts lengthened 2" (5 cm), Pockets in side seams.

STRIPE ON SIDE FROM CONTRASTING FABRIC

Adding a running stripe at the sides of the pants looks great if the shirt or the jacket is from the same fabric as the stripe. The pattern pieces for the front and the back will need to be made narrower to allow for the stripe.

Draw a line, parallel to the grain line, from the waist to the bottom of the leg on both the front and the back. Cut the pattern apart on this line and overlap the pieces ¾" (2 cm) to make the pattern narrower. Cut two strips of contrasting fabric the length of the pants and 2" (5 cm) wide.

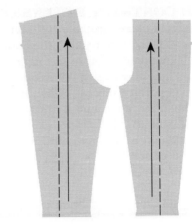

Sew the strip to the back and the front, right sides together, at the outside leg seams. If you wish to have side pockets, sew the pockets to the front side seams. Continue sewing the pants as described previously.

3/4" (2 cm) 3/4" (2 cm) 2" (5 cm)

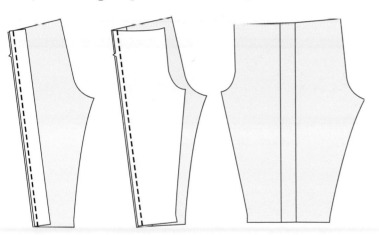

STITCHED WAIST ELASTIC

If you prefer to have a wider stitched elastic at the waist be sure to add 1" (2.5 cm) to the top of the waist when cutting out the pants or the shorts.

Sew the pants as previously described to the point of finishing the waist. At the waist, fold 1⅞" (4.5 cm) to the wrong side for the casing and press.

Cut a piece of 1½" (4 cm) wide elastic the following length:

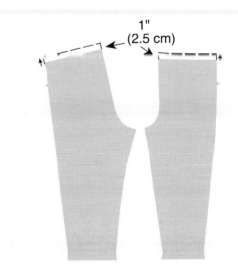

1" (2.5 cm)

XS	S	M	L	XL
19"	20"	21"	21½"	22½"
48 cm	51 cm	53 cm	55 cm	57 cm

Sew the elastic and the casing, following the instructions on Pages 47 and 48.

Add two rows of stitching through all layers ½" (1.3 cm) apart. Use a longer than medium stitch length and be sure to stretch the elastic to fit the fabric.

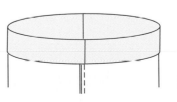

SHORTS WITH CONTRAST EXTENSIONS

To give the appearance of wearing another pair of shorts underneath, add a contrast extension to the bottom of the shorts. Make the extensions from a knit fabric such as single knit, fabric with Lycra or spandex and swimsuit fabric. On the shorts pattern pieces, measure the bottom edge of the front and the back and deduct 1½" (4 cm). Cut two pieces of fabric that length and 4" (10 cm) wide. Fold each end, right sides together, and sew the ends. Turn right side out and press.

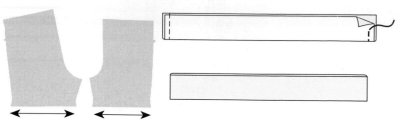

On the shorts, fold up 1" (2.5 cm) hem and press. Fold the legs in half at the outside leg seam and mark with pins. Divide the bands in half with pins. Pin the band to the right side of the shorts, with all the raw edges together, matching the pins and the finished edges of the band at the outside leg seam. Sew close to the edge, stretching the band to fit, if necessary. Overcast the raw edges together. Fold up the hem, and sew close to the edge of the hem through all layers.

Basic T-shirt, Shorts with Contrast extensions, Pockets in side seams.

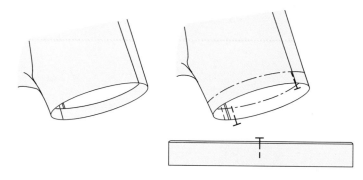

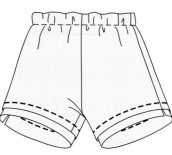

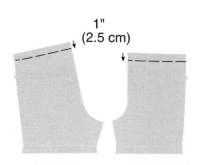

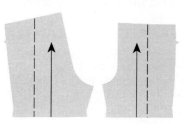

FLARED SHORTS

Girls love flared shorts, because they are a little dressier and very comfortable to wear. You will be using the pattern pieces for the shorts with minor adjustments. Trace Master pattern pieces 25 and 26, following the cutting line for the shorts.

On the front and the back, trim 1" (2.5 cm) at the waist. Draw a line from the waist to the bottom edge in the center of the waist, parallel to the grain line.

1"
(2.5 cm)

Cut the pattern apart on this line from the bottom edge to the waist. Place a piece of paper under the pattern. Spread the pattern apart 3" (8 cm) at the bottom edge, tapering to nothing at the waist. Tape in place. Draw a new grain line in the middle of the adjustment. At the bottom edge, draw a straight line from the inside leg to the outside leg seam and eliminate the hem extensions.

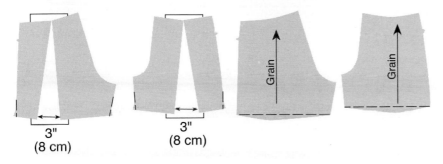

3"
(8 cm)

3"
(8 cm)

Cut out the shorts and sew the shorts as described previously to the point of finishing the waist.

The waist can be finished with elastic or a drawstring.

WAIST WITH DRAWSTRING

Overcast the raw edge of the waist. Mark buttonholes on the front 1" (2.5 cm) below the waist and ⅝" (1.5 cm) from the center front seam. Fuse small pieces of fusible interfacing to the wrong side of the front under the position of the buttonholes. Make the buttonholes.

Fold the waist ¾" (2 cm) to the wrong side and press. Sew close to the inner edge of the casing. Make a drawstring from the self fabric or use a purchased drawstring. Insert the drawstring into the casing through the buttonholes.

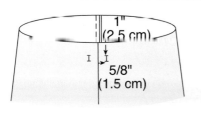

1"
(2.5 cm)

5/8"
(1.5 cm)

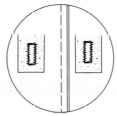

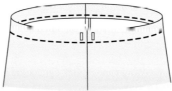

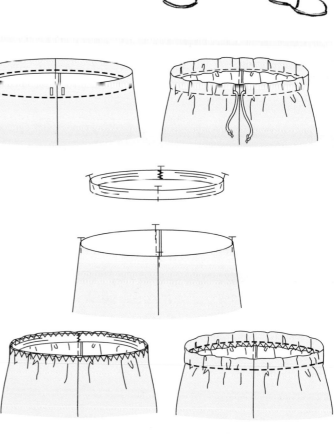

WAIST WITH ELASTIC

Cut a piece of ¾" (2 cm) wide elastic the following length:

XS	S	M	L	XL
18"	19"	20"	20½"	21½"
46 cm	48 cm	51 cm	52 cm	54 cm

Overlap the ends of the elastic ⅜" (1 cm) and sew them together. Divide the elastic and the waist into fourths with pins. Pin the elastic to the wrong side of the waist, matching the pins and the edge of the elastic even with the edge of the waist. Sew over the edge of the elastic and the waist, stretching the elastic to fit the waist; use a wide zigzag stitch or the serger (overlock) machine. Fold the elastic to the wrong side and sew through the elastic and the shorts ⅝" (1.5 cm) from the top edge of the waist, using a longer than medium stitch length.

Dresses & Skirts

Most girls think it is fun to dress up in a pretty dress or skirt. Girls want dresses and skirts which are comfortable and your best choice is a dress made from knit fabric and skirts with elastic at the waist. In this section, we will give instructions for cutting and sewing a T-shirt dress, straight skirt, gathered skirt and a tiered skirt. Make these extra special by adding lace, trims and ruffles.

T-SHIRT DRESS

You can make a pretty dress by using the T-shirt pattern pieces and adding a skirt. The dress has a dropped waist and a gathered skirt. You can make the dress with a ribbing neckband or you can use any of the T-shirt variations for the neckline and the sleeves, see the T-shirt instructions. For the dress bodice, use stretch knits only, such as single knit and interlock. For the skirt, knit or woven fabrics can be used, woven fabrics such as cotton types, lace, eyelet, satin, velveteen and baby cord and knits such as single knit, interlock and double knit.

Use Master pattern pieces:

1. T-shirt Front, use line for dress bodice
2. T-shirt Back, use line for dress bodice
3. T-shirt Sleeve
4. T-shirt Neckband or if using a neckline variation, choose pattern pieces accordingly.

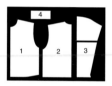

Trace the pattern pieces and on the front and the back, use the cutting lines for the **dress bodice.** The Master pattern does not include a pattern piece for the skirt. Use the measurements below and cut two. The length given allows for a 1" (2.5 cm) hem and a ⅝" (1.5 cm) seam allowance at the waist.

	XS	S	M	L	XL
Width					
	24"	25½"	27"	28½"	30"
	61 cm	65 cm	69 cm	72 cm	76 cm
Length					
	10"	11¼"	13¾"	15½"	17"
	26 cm	29 cm	35 cm	40 cm	43 cm

The finished length of the dress at the center back is as follows:

	XS	S	M	L	XL
	21"	23½"	27"	29½"	32"
	54 cm	59 cm	68 cm	75 cm	81 cm

Compare the finished length to the length you need and shorten or lengthen, if necessary. Cut out the dress, following the layouts.

Shirt with placket and faced neckline, Shirt is shortened and eyelet added to bottom edge, Tiered skirt, Hair bow.

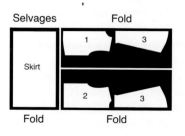

Dress with Long Sleeves
Fabric 60" (152 cm) Wide

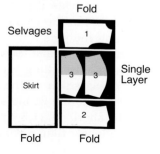

Dress with Short Sleeves
Fabric 60" (152 cm) Wide

54

Sew the dress bodice, following the T-shirt instructions.

Sew the side seams of the skirt. Sew gathering stitches on the waist of the skirt ⅝" (1.5 cm) from the edge and again in the middle of the seam allowance.

Divide the waist of the bodice and the skirt into fourths with pins. Pin the skirt to the bodice, right sides together, matching the center front, the center back, and the remaining pins to the side seams. Pull up the gathering stitches to fit the bodice, adjusting the gathers evenly. Sew the skirt to the bodice, using a ⅝" (1.5 cm) seam allowance and overcast the raw edges together. Overcast the bottom edge of the dress. Fold up the hem and sew close to the inner edge. If desired, hem by hand or use a blind hem stitch.

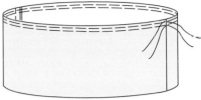

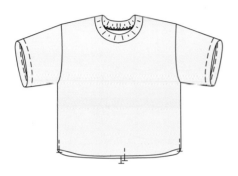
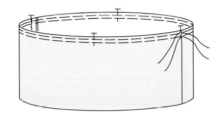

DRESS WITH SEAM AT WAIST

The basic dress, using the Master pattern, has a dropped waist, if you prefer you can make the dress with the seam at the waist. Trace the pattern pieces for the front and the back, following the lines for **dress bodice**. Shorten the front and the back bodice at the shorten and lengthen line 1½" (4 cm) for sizes XS and S and 2½" (6 cm) for sizes M, L and XL. Use the measurements for the skirt given on Page 54 and lengthen the skirt 3½" (9 cm) for sizes XS and S and 4½" (12 cm) for sizes M, L and XL.

Dress with seam at waist, Front placket and faced neckline, Headband with bow.

Sew the dress as described previously. Add elastic to the waist seam to make the dress fit closer to the body at the waist. Use ⅜" (1 cm) wide elastic and cut the elastic the following length. Or measure elastic around the child's waist so it feels comfortable.

XS	S	M	L	XL
19"	20"	21"	22"	23"
48 cm	51 cm	53 cm	56 cm	58 cm

Overlap the ends of the elastic and stitch together securely. Divide the elastic and the waist into fourths with pins.

Pin the elastic to the waist seam allowance on the bodice side, matching the pins and the edge of the elastic along the seam. Sew in the middle of the elastic, using a zigzag stitch and stretch the elastic to fit the fabric.

STRAIGHT SKIRT

A pull-on straight skirt is one of the easiest garments to make. You can use a firm knit or a woven fabric. Use knits such as single knit, double knit, sweatshirt fleece and woven fabrics such as broadcloth, twill, baby cord and lightweight denim. To make the pattern piece for the skirt, use the front pattern piece for the shorts and make the following adjustments.

Trace Master pattern piece 25 on the line for the shorts. Continue the center front line to the bottom edge. At the side, draw a perpendicular line from the bottom edge to the side. Check for the correct length of the skirt. The finished length of the skirt is the same as the shorts, see Page 46. Shorten or lengthen the skirt, if desired.

Cut out two pieces for the skirt, placing the center front on the fold of the fabric, the front and the back will be the same. Sew the pieces together at the side seams, using a **⅝" (1.5 cm)** seam allowance. Press the seams open. Finish the waist, following instructions for the pants and the shorts on Pages 47 and 48.

Overcast the bottom edge of the skirt. Fold up the 1" (2.5 cm) hem and press. Hem the skirt by topstitching or use a blind hem stitch.

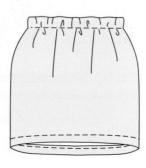

GATHERED SKIRT

A gathered skirt can be dressy or casual, depending on the type of fabric used. A ruffle can be added to the bottom edge to make it special. Use soft lightweight woven or knit fabrics such as challis, cotton, cotton types and cotton knits. The skirt has a casing with elastic at the waist.

To make a pull-on gathered skirt, cut two pieces of fabric the following length and width:

	XS	S	M	L	XL
Width					
	22"	24"	26"	28"	30"
	56 cm	61 cm	66 cm	71 cm	76 cm
Length					
	15"	17"	19"	21"	23"
	38 cm	43 cm	48 cm	54 cm	59 cm

Using these measurements the finished skirt length will be:

XS	S	M	L	XL
12"	14"	16"	18"	20"
30 cm	35 cm	40 cm	45 cm	51 cm

Shorten or lengthen the skirt, if necessary.

Pin the pieces, right sides together, and sew the short sides .

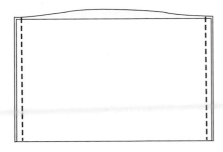

Overcast the top and the bottom edges of the skirt. At the waist, fold 1⅜" (3.5 cm) to the wrong side for the casing and press. Sew close to the edge, leaving an opening for inserting the elastic.

Cut a piece of elastic the length given for pants and shorts on Page 47. Attach a safety pin to one end of the elastic and thread the elastic into the casing through the opening. Overlap the ends of the elastic ⅜" (1 cm) and sew together. Finish sewing the casing seam. Distribute the gathers evenly. Sew across the width of the elastic at the center front, the center back and the side seams. Fold a 1" (2.5 cm) hem to the wrong side and sew close to the edge of the hem or hem with a blind hem stitch.

If you would like to make the skirt with a ruffle at the bottom edge, refer to Page 72 for adding ruffle.

Shirt with placket and collar, Short roll-up sleeves, Gathered skirt, hair bow.

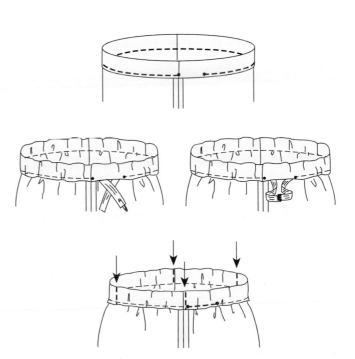

TIERED SKIRT

Choose light to medium weight fabrics such as cotton, crinkle cotton, handkerchief linen, lace, cotton knit or interlock. All three tiers can be made from the same fabric or each tier can be made from a different fabric. Small coordinated prints make a pretty skirt. You can add a special touch by adding lace or eyelet over the seams and at the bottom edge.

To make the tiered skirt, cut two pieces for each tier the measurements given below. The measurements include ⅝" (1.5 cm) seam allowances and hem, and 1⅜" (3.5 cm) is allowed at the waist for the casing. The finished length of the skirt is the same as the gathered skirt on Page 57.

TIER I - Cut 2

	XS	S	M	L	XL
Length					
	5½"	6"	6½"	7"	7½"
	14 cm	15 cm	17 cm	18 cm	19 cm
Width					
	15"	16"	17"	18"	19"
	38 cm	41 cm	43 cm	46 cm	48 cm

TIER II - Cut 2

	XS	S	M	L	XL
Length					
	5"	5½"	6½"	7"	7½"
	13 cm	14 cm	17 cm	18 cm	19 cm
Width					
	22"	24"	25"	27"	28"
	56 cm	61 cm	64 cm	69 cm	71 cm

TIER III - Cut 2

	XS	S	M	L	XL
Length					
	6"	7"	7½"	8½"	9"
	15 cm	18 cm	19 cm	21 cm	23 cm
Width					
	33"	36"	38"	40"	43"
	84 cm	92 cm	97 cm	102 cm	109 cm

T-shirt, Self fabric neckband, Short roll-up sleeves, purchased appliqués, Tiered skirt.

Sew the two sections for each tier, right sides together, at the short sides. Divide each tier into fourths and mark with a water soluble pen.

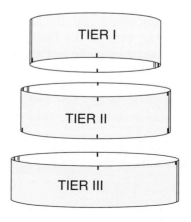

TIER I

TIER II

TIER III

Sew gathering stitches on the top edge of tier II and tier III, ⅝" (1.5 cm) from the edge and again in the middle of the seam allowance. Pull up the gathering stitches to gather the tiers.

Pin tier II to tier I, right sides together, matching the seams and the marks. Pull up the gathering stitches to fit, adjusting the gathers evenly. Sew the tiers together, using a ⅝" (1.5 cm) seam allowance.

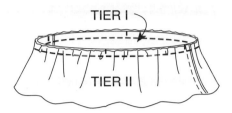

Pin tier III to tier II, right sides together, matching the seams and the marks. Pull up the gathering stitches to fit, adjusting the gathers evenly and sew the tiers together, using a ⅝" (1.5 cm) seam allowance.

Overcast the seam allowances together. Finish the waist, following the procedures for Pants and Shorts on Pages 47 and 48. At the bottom edge of the skirt, fold a double ¼" (6 mm) hem and press. Sew close to the edge of the hem.

If you wish to add lace at the seams, use ¼" - ¾" (6 mm - 2 cm) wide lace with one edge scalloped. Pin the lace to the bottom of each tier with the scalloped edge overlapping the seam. Sew the lace to the skirt close to the straight edge, overlapping the lace at one seam. If desired, add lace to the bottom edge. Overlap the straight edge of the lace, covering the hem stitches and sew on the lace close to the edge.

If you prefer to have the lace in the seams of the tiers, baste the lace to the top edge of tier II and tier III before sewing the gathering stitches. Gather the tiers and the lace in one step.

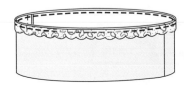 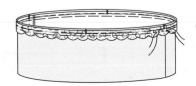

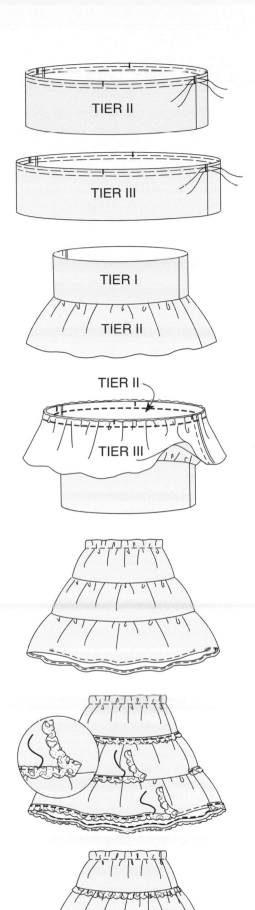

Sleep Wear

Nightshirts and pajamas can be very simple or they can be as elaborate as you wish by adding ruffles and appliqués. A nightshirt, nightgown, or pajama top can be made, using the pattern pieces for the T- shirt or the sweatshirt. Pajama bottoms can be made using the pattern for the pants. If using the T-shirt pattern, make the nightshirt or the pajamas from single knit or interlock. If using the sweatshirt pattern, use firm knits and woven fabrics, or for warmer sleep wear, use flannel or sweatshirt fleece.

T-shirt Master pattern pieces:
1. T-shirt Front
2. T-shirt Back
3. T-shirt Sleeve
4. T-shirt Neckband

Sweatshirt Master Pattern pieces:
13. Sweatshirt Front
14. Sweatshirt Back
15. Sweatshirt Sleeve
16. Sweatshirt Neckband
17. Sweatshirt Cuff

NIGHTSHIRT

Trace the pattern pieces. Adjustments need to be made on both the front and the back pattern pieces for the length and the width. To add width to the bottom edge of the front and the back, mark 1" (2.5 cm) at the sides. Lengthen the front and the back the following amount for an ankle length nightshirt:

Size	XS	S	M	L	XL
	15"	16"	18"	19½"	21"
	38 cm	41 cm	46 cm	50 cm	54 cm

Draw a new side seam from the underarm to the lengthened bottom edge, through the mark at the side.

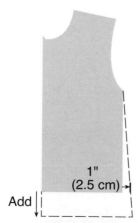

Cut out the nightshirt, following the layouts. Sew the nightshirt, following the instructions for the T-shirt or the sweatshirt. If you wish to add a ruffle to the bottom edge, refer to Page 72 for adding ruffles.

Nightshirt
Fabric 60" (152 cm) Wide

Fold

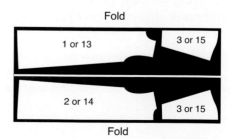

Fold

60

SHIRT TAIL HEMLINE

This is an easy adjustment you can make at the bottom edge of the nightshirt. At the bottom edge and at the side seam, measure and mark 7" (18 cm) as illustrated. Measure diagonally from the corner 3½" (9 cm) and mark. Draw a curved line connecting these three marks. Finish the hem before sewing the side seams. Overcast the bottom edge, fold a ¼" (6 mm) hem and sew close to the edge of the hem.

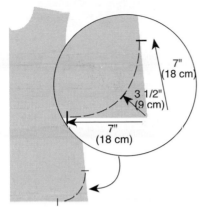

**Nightshirt (from sweatshirt),
Shirt-tail hemline, Pocket.**

POCKET

If you wish to add a kangaroo pocket to the nightshirt, use Master pattern piece 18. To mark the pocket placement, mark the bottom edge of the sweatshirt or the T-shirt from the Master pattern to the front. This will be the placement for the bottom edge of the pocket. Be sure to sew on the pocket before sewing the garment together.

On the pocket at the pocket openings, fold ¾" (2 cm) to the wrong side and press. Fold under the raw edge and press. Sew close to the edge. Fold all the raw edges of the pocket ¼" (6 mm) to the wrong side and press.

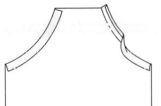
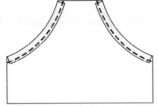
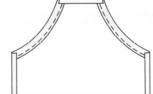

Place the pocket on the front with the right sides up, the bottom of the pocket along the placement marked, and the center of the pocket along the center front. Topstitch the pocket to the front close to the side, top and bottom edges. Reinforce the pocket opening by stitching as illustrated.

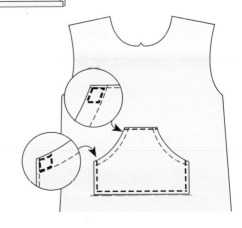

NIGHTGOWN WITH YOKE

As a variation, you can make a nightgown with a front and a back yoke. Trace the pattern pieces and follow instructions for nightshirt on Page 60 for changing the pattern pieces. On the front and the back pattern pieces, measure 1½" (4 cm) above the bottom of the armhole and draw horizontal lines to the center front and the center back. Cut the pattern apart on these lines and add ⅝" (1.5 cm) seam allowances to the front and back yokes and to the lower front and back. Add 3" (8 cm) to the center front and center back of the lower front and back.

Nightgown with yoke (from T-shirt), Cuffs.

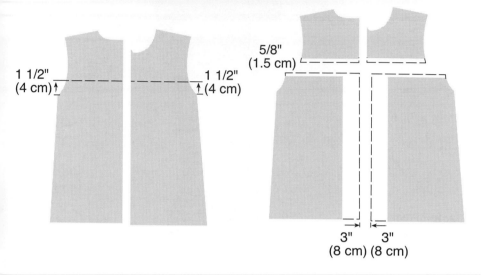

Cut out the nightshirt, placing the center front and the center back on the fold of the fabric. Sew gathering stitches on the lower front and back at the yoke seams ⅝" (1.5 cm) from the edge and again in the middle of the seam allowance.

Pin the front yoke to the lower front, right sides together, matching the center front. Pull up the gathering stitches to fit the yoke, adjusting the gathers evenly. Sew the yoke to the front and overcast the seam allowances together. Sew the back yoke to the lower back, using the same procedure. Sew the nightgown as described for T-shirts or sweatshirts.

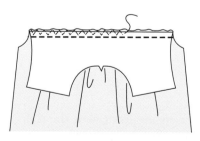

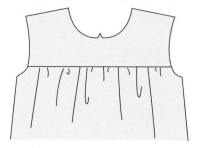

GATHERED LACE OR RUFFLE IN YOKE SEAM

If you wish to add gathered lace or a ruffle to the front yoke seam, use pregathered lace or make a ruffle.

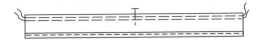

To make a ruffle, cut a piece of fabric 2½" (7 cm) wide and one and a half times the length of the yoke seam. Finish one edge of the ruffle with a narrow hem. Mark the center of the ruffle. Sew gathering stitches on the unfinished edge of the ruffle ⅝" (1.5 cm) from edge and again in the middle of the seam allowance.

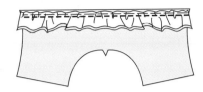

Pin the ruffle to the front yoke, right sides together, matching the mark to center front and with the ends of the ruffle at the armholes. Pull up the gathering stitches to fit the yoke and adjust the gathers evenly. Sew the ruffle to the yoke, using a ⅝" (1.5 cm) seam allowance.

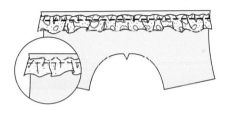

If using pregathered lace, place the right side of the lace to the right side of the yoke, placing the seam line on the lace ⅝" (1.5 cm) from the edge of the yoke and sew ⅝" (1.5 cm) from the edge.

Pin the yoke to the lower front, matching the center front and sew the yoke to the front in the previous line of stitching. Trim the seam allowance and overcast the raw edges together. Continue sewing the nightgown as described previously.

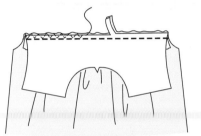
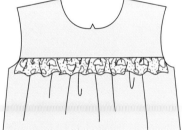

PAJAMAS

If you wish to make pajamas, use Master pattern pieces for the pants for the pajama bottoms, and use the pattern pieces for the T-shirt or the sweatshirt for the pajama top. Refer to the appropriate section for pattern pieces and sewing. Cut out the pajamas, following the layouts.

Shirt with Long Sleeves and Pants
Fabric 60" (152 cm) Wide

Fold

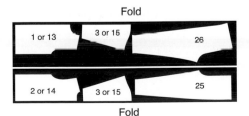

Fold

Shirt with Short Sleeves and Shorts
Fabric 60" (152 cm) Wide

Fold

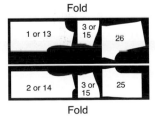

Fold

Use soft elastic for the waist, non-roll or stiff elastic is not suitable for sleep wear. If you wish to add cuffs to the bottom edge of the legs, refer to Page 49.

PAJAMA PANTS WITHOUT SIDE SEAMS

The side seams on the pants can be eliminated when making pajama bottoms and the adjustment is easy. Trace the pattern pieces for the pants. On the outside leg seam of the front, mark 1" (2.5 cm) at the waist and at the bottom of the leg. Overlap the back over the front, placing the back at the marks and tape in place. Draw a line, connecting the inside legs at the bottom edge. Fold the pattern piece in half, matching the bottom edge and crease. The crease will be the new grain line for the pants.

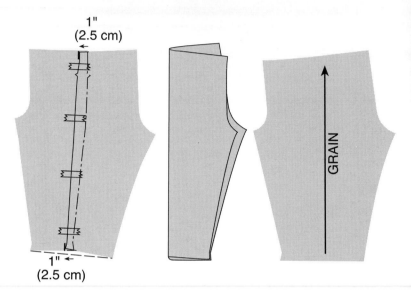

Cut out the pants. Sew the pants, right sides together, at the center front and the center back seams. Pin the pants, right sides together, at the inside leg seams, matching the center front seam to the center back seam. Sew from the bottom of the inside leg seam on one leg to the bottom edge of the other leg. Finish the waist and the bottom of the legs as described previously.

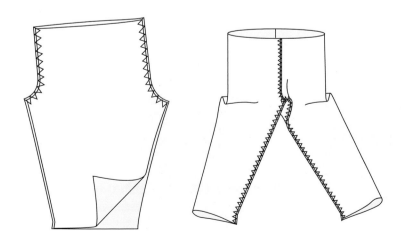

Pajama Top (from T-shirt), Cuffs, Pajama pants without side seams, Leg cuffs.

Design Changes

The fun of sewing is to be able to change the look of a basic garment, to create a "one-of-a-kind". This section is full of ideas for easy ways to add that personal touch.

COLOR BLOCKING

Color blocking gives you a wonderful opportunity to be creative and to use your imagination. The possibilities are endless. It is fun to do and it is very easy. Color blocking can be done on T-shirts, sweatshirts, jackets, pants and shorts. The simplest way to do color blocking is to use a different color fabric for each part of a garment, for example, the front one color, the back another color and the sleeves a third color. It is fun to work with fabric with stripes; use different sizes of stripes, or cut a pattern piece with the stripes in the opposite direction on part of the garment.

To color block, start with a simple design. Think of it as a puzzle, the fewer and the larger the pieces, the easier your garment will be to put together. When you are making your own designs, bear in mind that horizontal and vertical designs are the easiest to make and can be placed at any position. After you have made your first design, you will see how easy it is.

Choose the garment you want to make and select the pattern pieces, following the basic instructions for that particular garment. The designs presented in this book are to give you ideas. The measurements are approximate and you may want to vary the measurements. Design A, B, C, D and E can be made on T-shirts and sweatshirts. Design F is shown on a jacket, but could be used on a T-shirt or a sweatshirt. Some designs can be used on the front only or they can be used on both the front and the back.

CUTTING

When making a color blocked design that is different on the left and the right side of the garment, be sure to trace the pattern twice and mark the **right side of the fabric and the right and left** on the pattern pieces as illustrated. When cutting out the garment, place all pattern pieces with the marked side up on the right side of the fabric.

Sweatshirt, Stand-up collar with drawstring, Drawstring at bottom edge, Hemmed sleeves with elastic, Color blocking Design B, Pants, Stripe on side seam from contrasting fabric, Leg elastic.

Right Front — Right Side of Fabric

Left Front — Right Side of Fabric

Left Back — Right Side of Fabric

Right Back — Right Side of Fabric

BASIC INSTRUCTIONS FOR COLOR BLOCKING USING
Design A

Trace the pattern pieces. On the front pattern piece, draw a line perpendicular to the center front 1" (2.5 cm) above the underarm. Draw another parallel line below this line at the position desired. Extend the grain line so it will be on each piece. If you wish, make marks across the lines for matching, to make it easier when sewing. Number the pieces in the order they will be sewn together.

Cut the pattern apart and add seam allowances to the new cutting lines. Add ¼" (6 mm) seam allowance or if you plan to topstitch the seams, add ⅝" (1.5 cm) seam allowances. Cut out all the pattern pieces. Sew the front pieces together, sewing 1 to 2 and 3 to 2. Refer to the section of the particular garment you are making for sewing the garment.

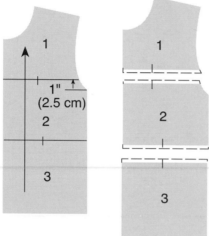

Design B

Trace the pattern pieces. On the front pattern piece, draw a line perpendicular to the center front 1" (2.5 cm) below the underarm and draw a parallel line 2" - 3" (5 cm - 8 cm) below this line. Draw the lines on the sleeve, using the same measurements. Number the pieces in the order they will be sewn and add the marks for matching. Cut the pattern apart and add the seam allowances.

Sweatshirt, Color blocking Design B.

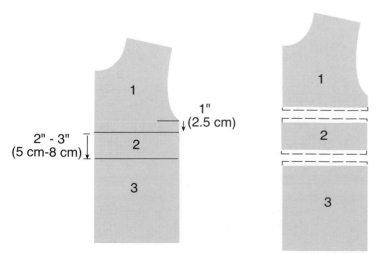

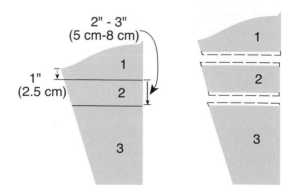

Design C

Trace the pattern pieces. On the front pattern piece, divide the side seam in half and draw a line perpendicular to the center front. Draw a parallel line 1½" (4 cm) above this line. Cut the pattern apart and add the seam allowances to the cut edges and to the center front on the upper part. Place the inset and the lower part on the fold.

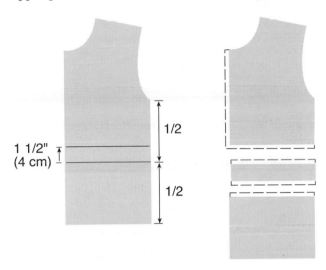

Design D

Trace the pattern piece for the front to make a complete front. On the left front, mark on the shoulder ½" (1.5 cm) from the neckline. Draw a line parallel to the center front from the shoulder to the bottom edge. Draw a parallel line 1½" (4 cm) from this line, toward the armhole. Cut the pattern apart on these lines and add the seam allowances.

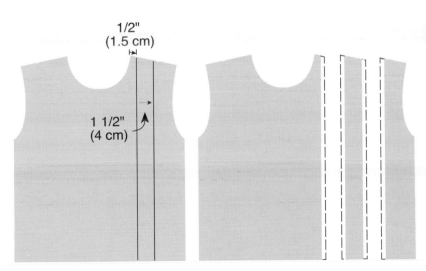

Sweatshirt, Color blocking Design D, Pants, Leg cuffs.

Design E

Trace the pattern pieces for the front to make a complete front. Mark ¾" (2 cm) below the shoulders at the armholes. Mark at the side seams 2" (5 cm) above the bottom edge. Draw two diagonal lines between these points. Number the pattern pieces in the order they will be sewn together. Add marks for matching. Cut the pattern apart on the lines and add the seam allowances. Sew 1 to 2, 3 to 4, and 3 and 4 to 1 and 2.

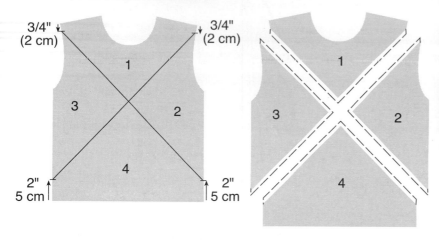

Shirt with placket and collar, Cuffs, Color blocking Design E.

Design F   (See photo on Page 48)

Trace the pattern piece to make a left and a right front. On the left front, mark on the center front 5" - 5½" (12 cm - 14 cm) below the neckline and mark on the armhole ¾" (2 cm) below the shoulder. Draw a line, connecting these marks. Draw another parallel line 2" (5 cm) below this line. Transfer the lower line to the right front. On the center front, mark 1" (2.5 cm) above the bottom edge. Draw a line from the center front to the side seam, this line should be parallel to the line on the upper part of the pattern. Draw a parallel line 2" (5 cm) above this line.

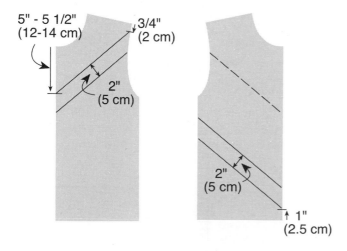

Label the pieces in the order they will be sewn and add marks for matching. Cut the pattern apart on the lines and add the seam allowances.

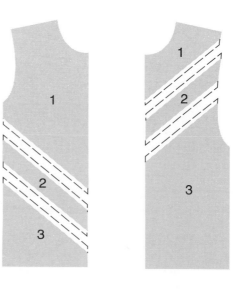

KWIK & EASY DETAILS

Add a few details and make the outfit very special. Additional neckline variations to make on T-shirts and pull-overs are included, as well as ruffles, ribbon design, decorative hand stitches and much more to personalize any garment.

DOUBLE RIBBING NECKBAND

A double ribbing neckband makes an attractive finish on a T-shirt or a sweatshirt. Use two contrasting colors of ribbing. Cut one neckband, using the pattern piece and cut the other neckband ¾" (2 cm) wider. Sew the center back seam of each neckband. Fold each neckband double, wrong sides and raw edges together.

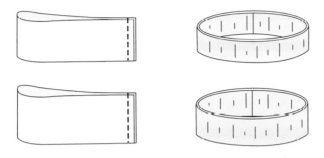

Pin the narrower neckband over the wider neckband, matching the seams and with the raw edges even. Sew the neckbands together with a wide zigzag stitch. Place the narrower neckband to the right side of the neckline and apply the neckband as described on Page 16.

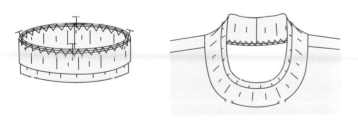

PATCHED NECKBAND

There is finally a way to use up all the small pieces of ribbing you have been saving. Cut pieces of different color ribbings the same width as the neckband pattern piece, and sew them together. Press the seams open. Fold the pieced neckband in half and cut out the neckband, using the pattern piece. Sew the neckband to the shirt as described on Page 16.

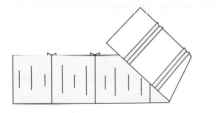

Sweatshirt, Double ribbing neckband.

Sweatshirt, Hemmed sleeves, Drawstring, Patched neckband, Appliqué.

NECKBAND WITH CONTRAST INSET

If you prefer, you can made a contrast inset at the center front of the neckband, the inset can be cut from a knit or a woven fabric. Cut the inset 2" (5 cm) long and the same width as the neckband. Cut the ribbing neckband ½" (1.3 cm) shorter than the pattern piece.

Sew the inset to the ribbing neckband and press the seams open. Apply the neckband as described on Page 16.

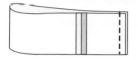

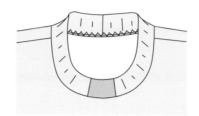

PATCHED FABRIC

Making a garment from patched fabric makes it an original which kids will love. Use your scrap pieces of fabric or purchase as many different fabrics as you wish to use. For approximate amount of fabric to purchase, divide the number of different fabrics into the amount of fabric given, for the particular garment you are going to make.

Cut the fabric into strips the same width. Cut the pieces into squares or rectangles or some of each. The pieces do not need to be the same size. Sew the pieces together into strips. Then sew the long strips together and cut out the garment.

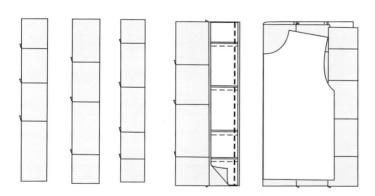

Pull-over, Drawstring, Patched fabric, Hemmed sleeves with elastic, Stand-up collar with drawstring, Decorative hand stitches.

OVERLAYS

Overlays give the appearance of color blocking, but are easier and faster to make. With overlays, you do not cut the pattern pieces apart, the contrasting pieces are placed on top of the garment and topstitched, and it is done before you sew the garment together. For the overlays, use lightweight woven fabrics, such as cotton, cotton blends, or nylon windbreaker fabric.

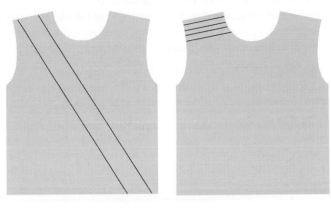

On the pattern piece, draw the size and the shape of the overlay and add the seam allowances, see the illustrations for suggestions. Cut out the overlays from contrasting fabrics. Fold under the raw edges and press. Pin the overlays to the garment with the right sides up and topstitch close to the edges.

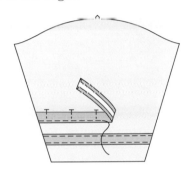

If you wish to have an overlay at the shoulders, sew the shoulder seams first, then sew the overlay over the shoulders.

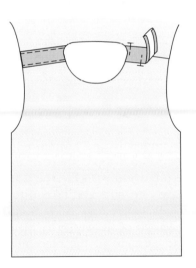

PATCHES, LABELS AND EMBLEMS

Children love labels and patches on their clothes. Most fabric stores have a good selection of decorative labels and emblems in a variety of sizes, colors and shapes. These can be sewn to the garment with hand stitches or by machine. You can also make your own labels and decorative patches from fabric. Look for a fabric with an interesting design and cut out the patch from the fabric, adding ¼" (6 mm) extra all the way around. Fold under the raw edges and press. Topstitch the patch to the garment close to the edges.

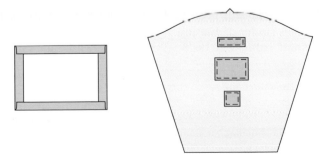

DECORATIVE HAND STITCHING

If you wish to add extra interest to a garment, use washable yarn and make hand stitches over the seams and the outside edges after the garment is completed.

Whip stitch: Make the stitches approximately ½" (1.3 cm) long and ⅝" (1.5 cm) apart. To whip stitch over a seam, come up at A, go down at B and up at C.

To whip stitch over the edge, come up at A, bring yarn over the edge and come up at B, continue until the edge is completed.

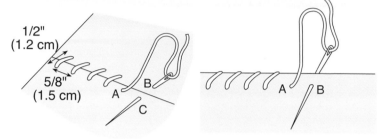

Blanket stitch: This stitch is like a buttonhole stitch. Start at the outside edge, bring needle up at A, make a loop, bring the needle through the loop and pull so the yarn lays along the outside edge. Repeat until the edge is completed. Make the stitches ¼" (6 mm) deep and ⅜" (1 cm) apart.

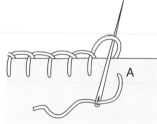

RUFFLES

Ruffles can be added to the bottom edges of T-shirts, dresses, skirts, pajama tops, short or long nightshirts. Ruffles can be any width. Decide the width of the ruffle you wish to have and add 1¼" (3 cm) to allow for a ⅝" (1.5 cm) seam allowance and ⅝" (1.5 cm) for the hem. Determine the length of the ruffle by measuring the bottom edge of the garment at the placement of the ruffle, and cut the ruffle approximately one and a half times that measurement. If using soft lightweight woven fabrics, the ruffle can be cut twice the measurement of the bottom edge.

Be sure to check for the correct length of the garment. The garment will need to be shortened the width of the finished ruffle, deducting ⅝" (1.5 cm). For example, if the finished ruffle will be 3" (7.5 cm), shorten the garment 2⅜" (6 cm).

Sew the short sides of the ruffle into a circle, right sides together.

Jacket with button closure, Round neckline, Side pockets, Hemmed sleeves, Decorative hand stitching.

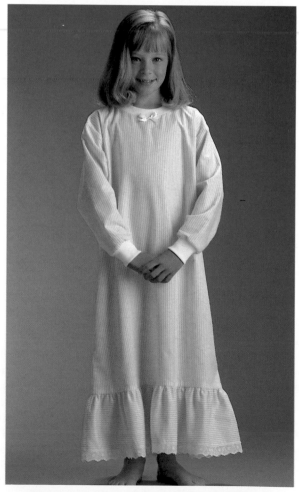

Nightshirt (from Sweatshirt), Ruffles.

Finish one side of the ruffle, using one of the following methods: For knit fabrics, overcast the raw edge and fold the hem along the overcasting to the wrong side and stitch. If using woven fabric, fold a double narrow hem and stitch.

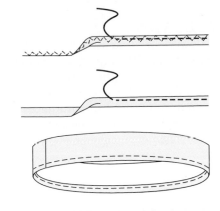

Divide the ruffle and the bottom edge of the garment into fourths with pins or mark with a water soluble pen. Sew two rows of gathering stitches, one on the seam line and one in the middle of the seam allowance. Pull on the bobbin threads to gather the ruffle.

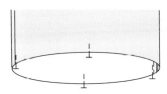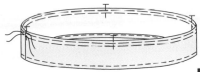

Pin the ruffle to the garment, right sides together, matching the pins. Sew the seam, using a ⅝" (1.5 cm) seam allowance. Overcast the raw edges together.

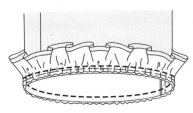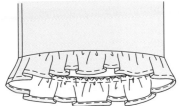

LACE MOTIFS

Lace motifs can be purchased in a variety of sizes, in single designs or in pairs to be used for the left and the right side of the garment. Lace motifs can also be cut from lace fabric, cut out the lace motif, following the heavy thread outlining the design.

Place the lace motif to the garment with the right sides up. Place a piece of "tear-away material" on the wrong side under the position of the motif and sew around the edges, using a medium zigzag width and a shorter than medium stitch length. Remove the "tear-away material". If desired, trim away the fabric under the lace motif, close to the stitches.

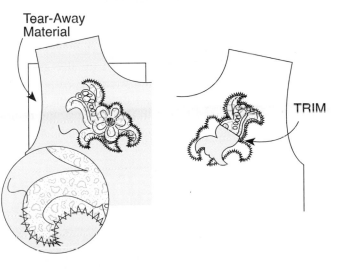

Basic T-shirt, Self fabric neckband and waistband, Lace motif.

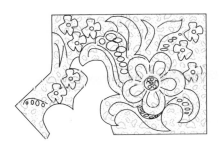

Tear-Away Material

TRIM

RIBBON FLOWER

Trace the flower on "tear-away" material. The ribbon flower should be applied to the garment before sewing the garment together. Place the "tear-away" material with the traced design on the wrong side of the garment at position desired and stitch over the lines with a straight stitch to transfer the design to the right side of the fabric.

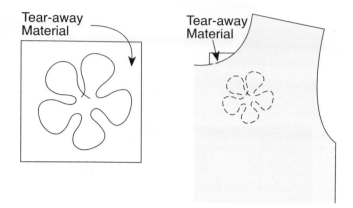

Tear-away Material

Tear-away Material

Use one ⅜" (1 cm) wide ribbon, or use two contrasting color ribbons. If using two ribbons, place the ribbons together and treat as one. Start at the center of the flower, fold under the end of the ribbon, guide the middle of the ribbon along the stitching line and sew in the center of the ribbon. Remove the "tear-away" material.

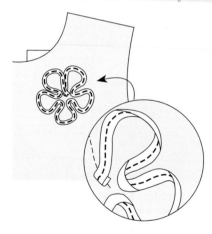

Sweatshirt, Ribbon flower, Puffed heart.

Ribbon Design

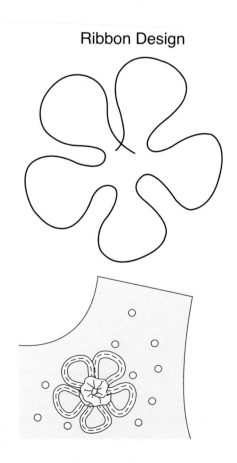

To make the center for the design, use the same ribbon or a wider ribbon can be used. Sew gathering stitches very close to one edge of the ribbon. Pull up the gathering stitches to gather and shape into a circle. Attach to the center of the design with hand stitches. If you wish you can attach a purchased flower in the center of the design. Add a few pearls, jewels or pretty buttons to embellish the design.

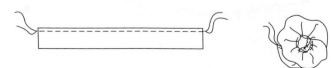

PUFFED HEART

Trace the heart. Cut out two hearts and mark the stitching line. Sew the hearts together, leaving an opening for turning and stuffing. Clip the seam allowances and turn right side out. Finger press the seam allowance open. Stuff the heart with polyester filling. Close the opening with hand stitches. Attach the heart at placement desired by sewing a button to the center or attach heart with hand stitches and glue a jewel to the center of the heart.

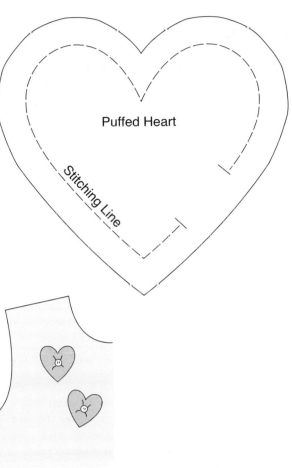

Puffed Heart

Stitching Line

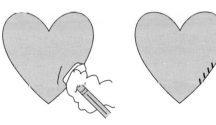

TRIM

Trims come in a variety of widths and you can use any width, depending on the placement of the trim on the garment. If you are using the trim to cover a curved seam on the garment, use narrow trim or bias tape. To cover the shoulder seams and the armhole seams, use a single fold bias tape, pin over the seams and sew close to both edges of the bias tape. Apply the tape to the shoulders before finishing the neckline, and apply to the armholes before sewing the side seams. See photo on Page 30.

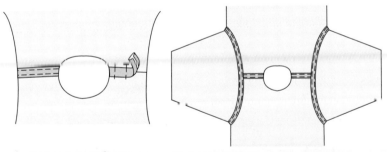

APPLIQUÉS

Appliqués make fun decorations for children's clothes. They can be used on T-shirts, sweatshirts, windsuits, and pants, in fact on almost everything. Use your imagination to decorate and personalize any outfit.

Appliqués can be applied to both knit and woven fabric. You can use scrap pieces of knit or woven fabric for the appliqués. Coordinate an outfit with an appliqué, for example, if you are making a T-shirt and pants, and you would like to have an appliqué on the T-shirt, use the pants fabric for the appliqué. Appliqués can be made from one color fabric or add other colors for detail areas. Buttons, rickrack, narrow ribbons, studs and jewels and any trim can be used to add detail to the appliqué. There are a number of different ways to do appliqués. The following are instructions for the two methods most commonly used.

Jacket with button closure, Hood, Side hemline slits, Appliqués.

METHOD I

USING PAPER BACKED FUSIBLE WEB

Making appliqués using paper backed fusible web is one of the easiest methods. Remember, when using this method, the finished appliqué will be the mirror image of the design. Select the fabric for the appliqué. Trace the design to the paper side of the fusible web. Place the rough side of the paper (side with glue) on the wrong side of the appliqué fabric and fuse. Cut out the appliqué. Peel off the paper backing. Fuse the appliqué to the garment at position desired.

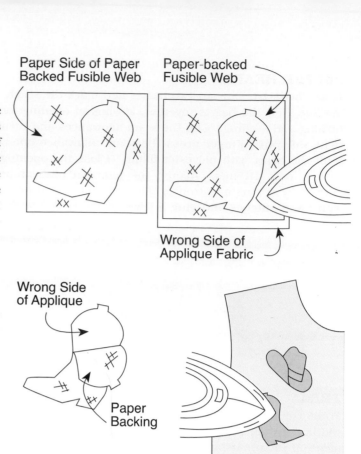

Stabilize the garment under the position of the appliqué, to prevent puckering when sewing on the appliqué. For stabilizing, use paper or especially made "tear-away" material. Cut the stabilizing material larger than the appliqué area. To hold the stabilizing material in place, pin, baste, or secure it with transparent tape.

Satin stitch over all the raw edges. To satin stitch, loosen the upper thread tension slightly and set the machine to a medium or slightly wider zigzag width and a very short stitch length. Test the stitches on a scrap piece of fabric, the zigzag stitches should cover the raw edges, but not be so close, that the thread piles up. When sewing, most of the zigzag stitches should be on the appliqué, sew with the needle just over the appliqué edge.

If there are any detail lines on the appliqué, sew them, using either a straight stitch or a narrow zigzag stitch. Some of the details may be sewn by hand, using embroidery stitches. Remove the stabilizing material on the wrong side.

APPLIQUÉS

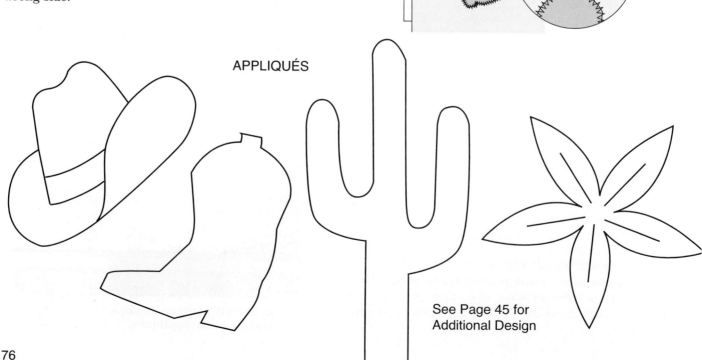

See Page 45 for Additional Design

An easy way to find designs for appliquéing, is to purchase a piece of fabric with a design that you like, it can be a flower or any other shape. Be sure to purchase enough fabric to get the complete design that you want. Or if you have a design on the fabric you are using for pants or shorts, you may want to cut out one design and use it as an appliqué on the shirt to coordinate the outfit.

Cut out the design, allowing extra fabric all around. Use paper backed fusible web and fuse to the wrong side of the fabric. Cut out the design. Remove the paper. Place the appliqué to the garment and fuse in place. Sew on the appliqué as described previously.

Wrong Side of Applique Fabric

Paper-backed Fusible Web

METHOD II

For this method, use a fusible interfacing to stabilize the appliqué fabric to prevent it from raveling. The interfacing will make the appliqué a little stiffer, but it makes it easier to sew.

Fuse interfacing on the wrong side of the fabric piece, which will be used for the appliqué. Transfer the design to the fabric, and cut out the appliqué.

Place the appliqué on the garment and secure with small pieces of fusible webbing, glue stick, or baste the appliqué to the garment with hand or machine stitches.

Place a piece of "tear-away" material on the wrong side of the garment, under the position of the appliqué, and pin or baste in place. Satin stitch over all the raw edges. If there are any detail lines on the appliqué, sew them, using either a straight stitch or a narrow zigzag stitch. Remove the stabilizing material on the wrong side.

APPLIQUE

Fusible Web

Tear-Away Material

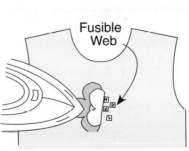

HAIR ACCESSORIES

Making hair accessories, is a fun and easy project you and your daughter or granddaughter can do together, save money and have one to match every outfit.

SCRUNCHY

You can use any light to medium weight soft fabric, such as broadcloth, challis, lace, single knit and interlock.

Cut a piece of fabric 4" x 20" (10 cm x 50 cm). Fold the strip, right sides together, and sew the long edge. Turn right side out and press. Cut a piece of ⅜" (1 cm) wide elastic 7" (18 cm) long. Insert the elastic into the strip and sew across the ends of the elastic and the strip. Overlap one end over the other and sew over the raw edges with a zigzag stitch.

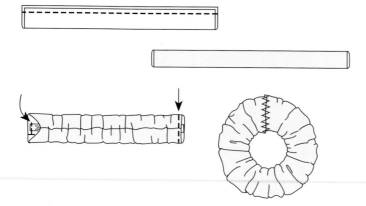

T-shirt dress, Self fabric neckband, Bows.

HEADBAND

For the headband, use knit fabrics with Lycra-spandex, such as swimsuit fabric and cotton-Lycra.
Cut a piece of fabric 3½" x 19" (9 cm x 48 cm) with the greatest degree of stretch along the strip. Fold the headband double, right sides together, and sew, using a medium zigzag width and a shorter than medium stitch length. Turn right side out and press. Overlap one end over the other and stitch over the raw edges with a zigzag stitch.

BOW

If you would like to add a bow to the headband, use the same fabric as the headband or use a contrasting knit or woven fabric. Cut a piece of fabric 6½" (17 cm) long and 5½" (14 cm) wide. Fold the piece, right sides together, and sew the long edge. Press the seam allowance open. Turn the bow right side out and place the seam in the middle. Fold the bow in half, placing the raw edges in the middle and stitch to keep in place. Cut a piece of fabric 1" x 2" (2.5 cm x 5 cm) for the knot. Fold the raw edges so they meet in the middle and press. Gather the bow in the middle and wrap the knot around the bow. Attach knot to bow with hand stitches.

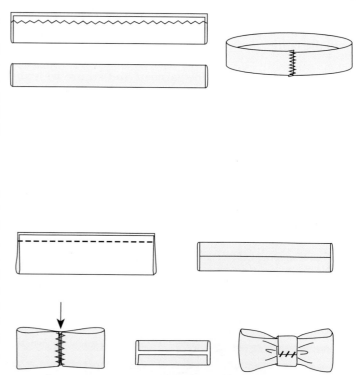

Attach the bow to the headband with hand stitches. These bows can also be used to decorate dresses and Tops.

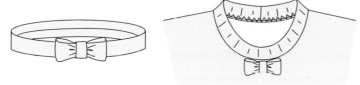

HAIR BOW

For this bow you will need a barrette, wire thread and lightweight woven fabric, such as broadcloth, handkerchief linen, batiste, sheer fabrics, lace, organza or voile.

Cut a piece of fabric approximately 4" x 20" (10 cm x 50 cm). If fabric ravels, hem both long sides of the strip with a narrow rolled hem, following these procedures: Fold ⅛" (3 mm) to the wrong side and stitch close to the edge with a straight stitch. Sew over the hem with a wider than medium zigzag width and a shorter than medium stitch length and be sure the zigzag is wide enough to catch the raw edges of the hem.

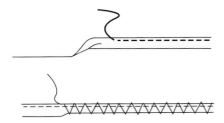

Remove the spring from the barrette. Divide the strip into five 4" (10 cm) spaces. Fold over one end to the first mark and wrap around the barrette with a wire thread. Form the remaining four pleats, wrapping around the barrette at each mark, one at a time. Return the spring to the barrette.

Jacket with zipper, neckband and drawstring - shortened 3" (8 cm), Color Blocking, Flared shorts, Hair Scrunchy.

Hair Bow.

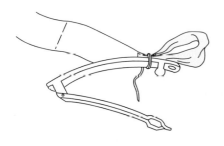
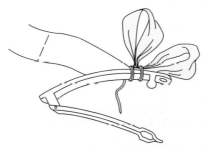
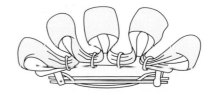

FABRIC REQUIREMENTS

Fabric requirements given for basic garments only.
If using variations or changing lengths, use the fabric requirements only as a guide.
Notions are not listed, purchase notions accordingly.
For the recommended fabrics, refer to the sections for each garment.

T-SHIRT–ALL STYLES
Fabric 60" (152 cm) wide:
LONG SLEEVES: Size XS–1 yd
(0.95 m), Size S–1⅛ yd (1.05 m),
Sizes M-L–1¼ yd (1.15 m),
Size XL–1⅜ yd (1.30 m).
SHORT SLEEVES: Sizes XS-S–
⅝ yd (0.60 m), Sizes M-L-XL–
¾ yd (0.70 m).
Contrast fabric for yoke:
⅜ yd (0.35 m).
Contrast fabric for placket and collar: ⅜ yd (0.35 m) of 45"
(115 cm) wide.

PULL-OVER & SWEATSHIRT
Fabric 60" (152 cm) or
45" (115 cm) wide:
LONG SLEEVES: Size XS–1 yd
(0.95 m), Sizes S-M–1⅛ yd (1.05 m),
Size L–1¼ yd (1.15 m),
Size XL–1⅜ yd (1.30 m)
SHORT SLEEVES: Sizes XS-S-M–
⅞ yd (0.80 m) Sizes L-XL–
1 yd (0.95 m).

PULL-OVER & SWEATSHIRT WITH HOOD
Fabric 60" (152 cm) wide:
LONG SLEEVES: Size XS–1 yd
(0.95 m), Sizes S-M–1⅛ yd (1.05 m),
Size L–1¼ yd (1.15 m),
Size XL–1⅜ yd (1.30 m).
SHORT SLEEVES: Sizes XS-S-M–
⅞ yd (0.80 m), Sizes L-XL–1 yd
(0.95 m).

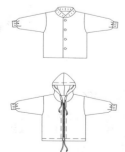

JACKET WITH LONG SLEEVES–ALL STYLES
Fabric 60" (152 cm) wide:
Size XS–1 yd (0.95 m),
Sizes S-M–1⅛ yd (1.05 m),
Size L–1¼ yd (1.15 m),
Size XL–1⅜ yd (1.30 m).
Fabric 45" (115 cm) wide:
Size XS–1⅜ yd (1.30 m),
Size S–1½ yd (1.40 m),
Size M–1⅝ yd (1.50 m),
Size L–1¾ yd (1.60 m),
Size XL–1⅞ yd (1.75 m).

PANTS AND SHORTS
Fabric 60" (152 cm) wide:
PANTS: Sizes XS-S–⅞ yd (0.80 m),
Size M–1 yd (0.95 m),
Sizes L-XL–1⅛ yd (1.05 m).
SHORTS: Sizes XS-S–½ yd (0.50 m),
Sizes M-L-XL–⅝ yd (0.60 m).
Fabric 45" (115 cm) wide:
PANTS: Size XS–1 yd (0.95 m),
Size S–1⅛ yd (1.05 m), Size M–1⅜ yd (1.30 m),
Size L–1¾ yd (1.60 m),
Size XL–1⅞ yd (1.75 m).
SHORTS: Sizes XS-S-M–¾ yd (0.70 m),
Size L–⅞ yd (0.80 m), Size XL–1 yd (0.95 m).

STRAIGHT SKIRT
Fabric 60" (152 cm) or 45" (115 cm) wide:
Sizes XS-S-M-L–½ yd (0.50 m),
Size XL– ⅝ yd (0.60 m).

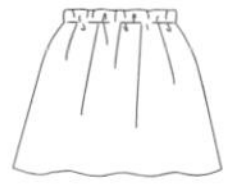

GATHERED SKIRT
Fabric 60" (152 cm) wide:
Sizes XS-S–½ yd (0.50 m), Sizes M-L–⅝ yd
(0.60 m), Size XL–¾ yd (0.70 m).
Fabric 45" (115 cm) wide:
Size XS–⅞ yd (0.80 m), Size S–1 yd (0.95 m),
Size M–1⅛ yd (1.05 m), Size L–1¼ yd (1.15 m),
Size XL– 1⅜ yd (1.30 m).

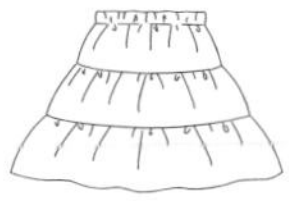

TIERED SKIRT
Fabric 45" (115 cm) wide:
Size XS–⅞ yd (0.80 m), Sizes S-M–1 yd
(0.95 m), Size L–1⅛ yd (1.05 m),
Size XL–1¼ yd (1.15 m).

T-SHIRT DRESS
Fabric 60" (152 cm) wide:
LONG SLEEVES: Size XS–1¼ yd (1.15 m),
Size S–1⅜ yd (1.30 m), Size M–1½ yd
(1.40 m), Size L–1⅝ yd (1.50 m),
Size XL–1¾ yd (1.60 m).
SHORT SLEEVES: Sizes XS-S–⅞ yd
(0.80 m), Sizes M-L–1 yd (0.95 m),
Size XL–1⅛ yd (1.05 m).

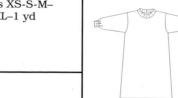

NIGHTSHIRT WITH LONG SLEEVES
Fabric 60" (152 cm) wide:
Sizes XS-S–1½ yd (1.40 m),
Size M–1¾ yd (1.60 m), Size L–1⅞ yd
(1.75 m), Size XL–2 yd (1.85 m).

PAJAMAS
Fabric 60" (152 cm) wide:
LONG SLEEVE TOP & PANTS:
Size XS–1⅞ yd (1.75 m), Size S–2 yd (1.85
m), Size M– 2⅛ yd (1.95 m), Size L–2¼ yd
(2.10 m), Size XL–2⅜ yd (2.20 m).
SHORT SLEEVE TOP & SHORTS:
Sizes XS-S–1¼ yd (1.15 m), Size M–1⅜ yd
(1.30 m), Sizes L-XL–1½ yd (1.40 m).

**Ribbing 28" (71 cm) wide: Neckband: 3" (8 cm),
Waistband: 5" (13 cm), Cuffs: 5" (13 cm).**